MEMORIES FROM THE OUT HOUSE MOUSE

THE PERSONAL DIARIES OF ONE B-17 CREW

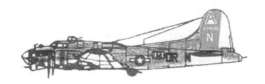

COMPILED AND TRANSCRIBED BY:
G. R. HARVEY

Trafford rev. 04/09/2024

 www.trafford.com

North America & international
toll-free: 844-688-6899 (USA & Canada)
fax: 812 355 4082

INTRODUCTION to the DIARIES:

The following are the combined personal diaries of the last World War II combat flight crew of the Boeing B-17 Flying Fortress named "Out House Mouse". Each of these diaries has been transcribed from the original or from a first generation copy of the original provided to me by the crewmember or his immediate family.

My father was 1Lt. E.J. ("Joe") Harvey, the pilot on this crew and it was the transcription of his diary that began this project. Lt. Harvey's notes were hand-printed in block capital letters and an effort has been made to retain that personality in this transcription. For each combat mission, Lt. Harvey also included carefully cut and folded newspaper accounts, which have also been transcribed and where possible, the source newspaper identified. An effort has been made to duplicate the newsprint type, column size and position as much as possible to retain the look of his original diary.

From his diary, I learned the names of the other members of his crew and their hometown at that time. Using that information, I've been able to locate all the members of the crew or their family. Six others have provided me with copies of their diary for which I am most grateful and I have included transcriptions of these diaries in this combined record. Because Lt. Harvey provided an entry for every day, even when not flying, and because his diary covers the greatest period of time, from the first of January through the middle of June 1945, his diary provides the date stamp and serves as the basis for all of the other records.

This combined chronological record includes the seven available records of all 9 members of this last combat crew of the "Out House Mouse". Thus, this record includes the diary of 2Lt. Phil Darby, the co-pilot, provided by Mr. Darby; the diary of 2Lt. Marty Raber, the bombardier who actually sent me his original diary and his scrapbook for my use in preparing this book; the diary of 2Lt. Paul Katz, the navigator for the crew, provided by his wife, Joan Katz; the diary of S/Sgt Niel C. Jorgenson, the crew's flight engineer, which has been provided by his daughter, Ms. Susan Lunt who also provided the computer scans of the photographs of the flight crew and their signatures at the beginning of this book. The remaining records are the "Mission Sheets" of the ball turret gunner, S/Sgt George H. Odenwaller and the diary of the tail-gunner S/Sgt Walter M. Limberger. Both of these gentlemen provided me with a hand-written reproduction of their diary. The last record of course is that of Lt. Harvey from which all of this has grown. Following the entries of the pilot and co-pilot, the entries from the other five diaries are arranged in a nose-to-tail order of that crewmember's position aboard the "Out House Mouse".

Each of these records is separated from the others by a break line (----) with each contributing member identified. In addition, the individual contributions also use a different type font. A sincere effort has been made to replicate the handwriting and format the diarist used in each of the original records. For example, while most of the diary authors established a format for reporting the specific important facts of their missions and recorded these facts in hand-printed letters, Paul Katz wrote his diary in long-hand using a narrative style and addressed it to his wife, Joan. Consequently, for Lt. Katz, I chose a script font to replicate the transcription of his diary. "Mission days" are preceded by a small pilot's wing prior to the diary date and conclude with the transcription of the newspaper account (or accounts) that Lt. Harvey had so carefully cut, folded, and pasted into his diary. Photographs from these articles have been electronically scanned and reproduced here.

The contributions of a few of the crew members warrant some additional explanation. The first crew member I contacted was Marty Raber, the bombardier. Marty told me that while technically he was always a member of Lt. Harvey's crew, after his first few missions, he was made lead bombardier of the squadron and consequently was usually with another crew in the lead aircraft. In addition, lead bombardiers had different mission assignments and may not have even been on the same missions as the "Out House Mouse". For this reason, Lt. Harvey's crew flew with a "Toggelier" who would set the bomb switches and bomb on command. Marty was obviously a good bombardier.

Using the dates and targets given in Marty's diary, I found that there were only a few dates where he obviously flew a different mission than that of the rest of his crew. Since his diary did not record the name or number of his aircraft, it is possible on the matching dates, while he was on the same mission, he may not have been on the same aircraft as the others. However, I feel his experiences are just as relevant to the events of that mission and have therefore "inserted" his diary entries in their proper place with the other crewmembers using the same nose-to-tail diary sequence. The few missions where he is clearly with another crew are noted.

Of the other crewmembers, Milton Lloyd the radioman, said he was required to copy an encrypted message in Morse Code every thirty minutes of each mission, and consequently he was very tired of writing and did not keep any records. The only other man in the waist, Al Kus, was the single waist gunner on Lt. Harvey's crew. Al told me that at that stage of the war, "the brass" had decided that it was not necessary to have two waist gunners on a B-17, consequently, he was the only waist gunner on the crew and he changed his position to operate the left- or right-hand waist gun as the situation required. In addition, after arriving in England, he was sent to a special school to learn the new system of jamming enemy radar with radio. During his tour, he usually flew in one of the three B-17's in the group which were equipped with this special jamming equipment. On these missions he was "available to handle the waist gun if necessary", but he wasn't usually aboard the "Out House Mouse". Al even gave his position on the back of the crew photograph as "Spot Jammer". While Al did keep a diary, his baggage was lost during his return home and so too his diary. When he received his draft copy of this book, he called me and thanked me for finally providing him with "his long lost diary". Al, I thank-you and you are included in this collection for from that conversation, I have included your recollection of the emergency landing in France on March 28, 1945.

These are the members of crew #8229 assigned the B-17 named the "Out House Mouse". While occasional discrepancies in the individual records of this crew are apparent, I have tried to contain my transcription comments to the clarification of terms and not to attempt to correct any errors as I did not want to detract from the original source material. My goal is to present these diaries as close to their originals as possible both in content and in presentation and at the same time, provide some insight into the meaning and consequences of their content.

At this time of the war, each aircrew member had to complete 35 combat missions to complete his combat tour. While each individual was a member of a crew, that crew did not always fly the same missions. For example, Lt. Darby was hospitalized for a time with an ear infection. Consequently his mission count fell about 7 behind the other members of his crew in March 1945. Also, as George Odenwaller had once told me, once aboard the aircraft, each member of the crew had a little different view of each mission due to his unique position and job in the aircraft. It is my sincere desire that by combining these records, the contributions of this one B-17 crew and its individual members can be better appreciated.

These diaries cover January through mid-June 1945. By this time, the 91st Bomb Group had distinguished itself as a tough, can-do bomber force that always got through and bombed their assigned targets. However, to do this, the 91st also distinguished itself with the highest loss rate. By the end of the war, 906 men were listed as killed or missing in action and approximately 1150 others as prisoners of war. In the four months of combat missions in these diaries, the 91st Bomb Group flew combat mission #278 through #340 where eight aircraft are listed as having been lost – a rate of two aircraft a month. The destinations of these missions include three missions to Berlin, two to the still controversial target of Dresden, and the disastrous final mission to Pilsen, Czechoslovakia. Their mission targets include oil facilities, marshalling yards, U-boat pens, airfields, rail centers and bridges. Following the end of the war in Europe May 8, 1945, several additional missions were flown to evacuate 2,454 allied POW's and to show ground personnel the war zone.

Alerted for redeployment to the Pacific in June 1945, the aircrews of the 91st began flying their surviving aircraft back to the USA carrying 10 passengers, their bags and any cargo the brass could load in the bomb bays instead of bombs. The remaining personnel returned to the USA on the *Queen Elizabeth* which docked in New York on June 30. The 91st Bombardment Group (Heavy) was deactivated on November 7, 1945, following the formal surrender of Japan on September 2, 1945.

I wish to acknowledge the help and encouragement of George Odenwaller who has been a personal historian of World War II, the 91st Bomb Group, and the "Out House Mouse" since the end of the war. His numerous historical society and museum memberships include a founding member of the American Air Museum in Britain at Duxford. In my very first telephone conversation with him, he immediately made me feel as though I was a member of his own family and near the end of that conversation told me to "…just tell me what you want to know." George has helped me locate the other crew members and provided me with the names and publishing information for a number of books that specifically mention the "Out House Mouse", my father, or other members of his crew that have helped me with this project. He and the other crew members have also provided me with the photographs in this book.

Finally, I extend a very sincere thank-you to all of these men and their families who have so freely shared this portion of their family's history with me - and I hope now - the world. Prior to starting this project, I had only my father's diary on which to try and understand his participation in the war. I believe that the fact that my father's diary even exists is proof of his sincere intent to share these experiences with his family, but to his dying day he suffered nightmares of this brief time in his life and he was never able to discuss the content of the diary he had so carefully prepared.

May the world never forget the sacrifices of all the men these few pages represent.

-grh-

Back, L-R
1st Lt. Elmer "Joe" Harvey, Pilot; 2nd Lt. Paul Katz, Navigator;
2nd Lt. Martin Raber, Bombardier; 2nd Lt. Phil Darby, Co-pilot;
Front, L-R
S/Sgt Niel Jorgenson, Engineer; S/Sgt Milton Lloyd, Radio;
S/Sgt. George H. Odenwaller, Ball Turret Gunner;
S/Sgt. Elmer Allen Kus, Wasit Gunner; S/Sgt. Walter Limberger, Tail Gunner

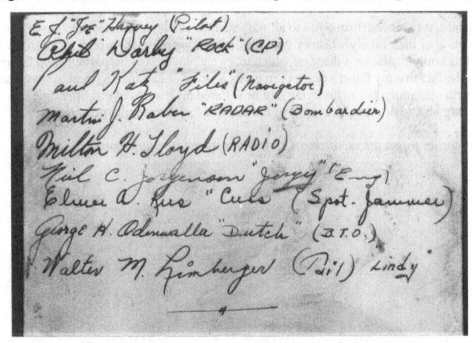

Signatures of Outhouse Mouse Flight Crew

[Mission Summary compiled using Lt. Harvey's diary - destinations in Germany unless otherwise shown:]

-1945-

# 1	Feb 6	Gotha	
# 2	Feb 9	Altenbeken	
	Feb 10		Scrubbed – 1st mission flown as a crew. Ships name "Out House Mouse".
# 3	Feb 14	Dresden	Due to SNAFU, we were thrown out of formation. Flew home alone.
# 4	Feb 15	Essen	Flak thru windshield and pants of Paul Katz – Navigator.
# 5	Feb 22	Stendal	.
# 6	Feb 23	Meiningen	Landed with only 200 gals left – Mission 11 Hours.
# 7	Feb 24	Hamberg	Only good landing in squadron.
# 8	Feb 27	Lipzig	Flew in "Out House Mouse" today.
# 9	Mar 1	Heilbronn	
#10	Mar 4	Ulm	
#11	Mar 10	Sinsen	
#12	Mar 12	Dillenberg	Milk Run. [easy mission - grh]
#12a	Mar 17	Bohlen	Landed with only 200 gals left – Mission 10 Hours.
#14	Mar 18	Berlin	ME-262 Jet attack. [This is the jet that looks like a T-33 – grh].
#15	Mar 22	Dorsten	Ike selected the target.
#16	Mar 24	Hengenld, Hol	
#17	Mar 28	Berlin	Emergency landing in France.
#18	Mar 31	Merseberg	A group coming off target ran thru us while on our bomb run.
#19	Apr 5	Grafenwohr	
#20	Apr 7	Kohlenbissen	
#21	Apr 10	Oranienburg	Mission #101 on "Out House Mouse" without an abort. Saw B-17 get direct flak hit and explode - no chutes were seen.
#22	Apr 11	Frieburg	
#23	Apr 13	New Munster	One formation dropped on a lower element and two ships were lost.
#24	Apr 16	Regensburg	
#25	Apr 17	Dresden	"Blood and Guts" badly hit right next to "Out House Mouse".
#26	Apr 18	Rosenheim	
#27	Apr 21	Munich	"Don't think you boys will have to come back to Munich".
#28	Apr 25	Pilsen, Chec	Last combat mission of 8th Air Force.
	May 7		Armistice announced. "Thank God that at least this much death and sadness had been brought to a halt." - EJH

-- Post War in Europe Flights --

	May 11	Lenz, Aust	Mission to fly out prisoners of war. "They were just skin and bones some barely able to walk … the ground was red with blood." - EJH
	May 13	Stettin, Ger	More POW evacuations – many had been POW's for over two years.

-- Flight Home --

	Jun 8	Valley, Eng	First leg of homeward trip with crew of 10 and 10 passengers. [Note: Lt. Harvey's normal crew was only 9-men - grh]
	Jun 9	Meeks Fld, Ice	Feathered #2, 3-hours out of Meeks due to broken governor.
	Jun 9	Goose Bay, Lab	#2 maintenance delayed 7A.M. take-off. Landed Goose Bay 21:40.
	Jun 10	Bradley Fld, Conn	Due to weather, redirected to Grenier Fld, NH.
	Jun 11	Bradley Fld, Conn	"Home at last and here we got milk for the first time since leaving the USA." - EJH

[This page intentionally left blank]

A PAGE A DAY

IDENTIFICATION
Name: E. J. HARVEY
My Weight is: 160 LBS   Height: 5' 11"
Color of Hair: DK. BWN   Color of Eyes: BLUE

- 1945 -
JANUARY 1
JUST BEEN ALERTED FOR SHIPMENT TO P.O.E. [point of embarkation – grh] AFTER BEING IN
THIS SPOT SINCE 4 DECEMBER 1944. THERE ARE MANY MORE INTERESTING PLACES THAN
LINCOLN, NEB. TO SPEND A MONTHS TIME. AND BESIDES IT HAS BEEN COLD AS HELL HERE
AFTER 5 YEARS IN THE SOUTH.

[Lt. Harvey refers to his earlier military experience. He enlisted in the 113th Cavalry in March 1939, and was
inducted into Federal Service January 13, 1941 and assigned to Camp Bowie, Texas. This was followed by
his officers training and commissioning at Fort Knox, Kentucky after which he was assigned as Company
Commander, Headquarters Company, 3rd Battalion, 44th Armored Regiment, Camp Campbell, Kentucky -
tanks. He was promoted to First Lieutenant in October, 1942 while at Camp Campbell. This information
was obtained from an Oscaloosa, Iowa newspaper clipping dated Friday, March 5, 1943. The last page of his
diary completes his military record prior to 1945 where Lt. Harvey lists: "Flying Training Aug 1943 - Jan
1945". - grh]

==

JANUARY 2
UP EARLY TO PACK LUGGAGE TO BE AT ORDERLY ROOM AT 1300 FOR SHIPMENT. MEN AND
OFFICERS LEAVE LINCOLN, A.A.F. [Army Air Field - grh] AT 1600 HOURS FOR P.O.E. TRAIN, AS
ALL ARMY TRAINS ARE, WAS ONE HOUR LATE. WE GOT NO SUPPER EITHER!

==

JANUARY 3
UP AT 8:00 FOR BREAKFAST. FIRST NITE[sic] ON TRAIN. GOT LOTS OF SLEEP AND MORE TO
COME I'M SURE. QUITE BOREING[sic] ALL DAY.

==

JANUARY 4
STILL ON THE TRAIN AND ALL OF US QUITE TIRED OF OUR RIDE. MEALS QUITE GOOD FOR
TROOP TRAIN. DULLEST TRIP I HAVE EVER HAD ON ARMY TRAIN.

THIS NITE[sic] I SLEPT WITH LOVELL SINCE THE MAN (LT. PITTS) ABOVE MY BUNK WAS
SICK AND PUT MOST OF HIS TUMMY ON MY BED. NOT SO DULL NOW!

==

JANUARY 5

STOPED [sic] AT GRAND CENTRAL STATION IN NEW YORK. NO ONE ALLOWED OFF TRAIN. WE GOT SANDWICHES ORANGE JUICE. TIME 0100 HOURS.

ARRIVED FT. MILES STANDISH ABOUT 1100 HOURS. FT. MILES STANDISH IS ABOUT 10 MILES FROM BOSTON.

WE WERE WELCOMED WITH A BAND AND THEN WALKED 5 MILES TO OUR QUARTERS WITH B-4 BAGS. QUARTERS QUITE COLD AND UNCOMFORTABLE.

[A B-4 bag is a soft-sided, fold-over piece of luggage with a large pouch on each side. These bags always seem to have room for one more item. Consequently they are usually quite bulky and hard to carry. These probably carried their dress uniforms and a few civilian cloths. - grh]

===

JANUARY 6

WE HAVE SPENT THIS DAY PROCESSING. MORE FORMS TO FILL OUT.

IT SEEMS THAT THE CREW HAS NO A-3 BAGS. THEY WERE NOT SHIPPED FROM LINCOLN. IT SEEMS. WE WILL GO OVERSEAS WITH NO FLYING EQUIPMENT.

[From Lt. Harvey's diary, the A-3 bags contained their flight equipment i.e. the nice warm fleece-lined leather jackets and boots for the 40 below temperatures typical at 15-20,000 feet. - grh]

===

JANUARY 7

LEFT FT. STANDISH, MASS. AT 2000 HOURS IN FULL FIELD GEAR FOR BOSTON, BY TRAIN. AT THE DOCKS THE 'ILLE DE FRANCE' [sic] WAS WAITING FOR US. QUITE A NICE AND HUGE SHIP.

[The following is the first diary entry for Lt. Phil Darby: - grh]

Full field packs in light snow – board train at Camp Miles Standish (30 miles from Boston). Arrive at Pier 8 at 2300. The band played "Officer of the Day" and "His Honor". Red Cross Ladies give each of us coffee and doughnuts. The sailors from our ship gave Raber [Martin Raber – bombardier See Jan 31 entry – grh] *and I a half pint of "Old Granddad". I stagger up the gang plank under the weight of pack and B4 bag. This is a big baby. I'm in Room A14 (A deck). A luxury liner before the war, the "Ille d'France" [sic] is sixth largest, 43,000 ton. Mounts 19 guns…they look good to me.*

[The following is the opening page and first diary entry for Lt. Paul Katz: - grh]

From Day to Day,
        By Lt. Paul Katz

To my darling wife, the history of my tour of duty in the E.T.O.
                    P.K.

Generally, overseas troop movements are made at night. Ours was no exception. We had been at Camp Miles Standish for two days looking for our A-3 bags and flying equipment which were lost enroute from Lincoln [Nebraska – grh] *when the order came through. We were to be packed and ready to leave for our point of embarkation at 2030 hours. At that time we boarded the train which took us to Boston harbor where the "Ile De France"* [sic] *was docked. The Red Cross was at the pier with coffee and doughnuts. After we had our coffee, we boarded ship and were shown to our staterooms. The quarters were nice. Especially after the barracks at Miles Standish. Since the hour was late and we were all tired from carrying our packs around, we went right to bed.*

[E.T.O. is the European Theater of Operations. At this time, Lt. Katz and Lt. Harvey are the only married members of this crew. Also of interest, is the fact that Lt. Katz wore glasses. At that time, all flight crew members were required to have 20/20 vision but, according to his wife Joan, Lt. Katz had completed his navigator training on B-24 Liberator's at Biggs Field before anyone seemed to notice his glasses. This grounded him for 3 months during which time he served as an instructor until the Army finally granted him a special dispensation – he may have been the only flight-crew member in the war who wore glasses. This delay also transferred him from the B-24 Liberator to the B-17 Flying Fortress. – grh]
==

JANUARY 8
1600 HOURS WE SET SAIL FOR THE UNITED KINGDOM. WE SPENT THE DAY GETTING SETTLED AND SEEING THE SHIP.

From the diary of Lt. Phil Darby:

We weigh anchor. The pilot guides us thru the sub nets and mine field. We have a boat drill and action stations. My Kapole Life preserver fits like an old harness. There is a poker game by my bunk. The sea's rough. Katz, the Navigator, loses his lunch. I must admit I have butterflies in my stomach. We're making 20 knots now, and the boards are creaking by my head.

[Note that they are sailing from Boston and the harbor is protected by "sub nets and mine field"! – grh]

From the diary of Lt. Paul Katz:

We had breakfast at 0800 this morning. There are four servings of each of the two meals. We are serving no. 2 which messes at 0800 and 1800 each day. We are still tied up in the harbor. At 1115 hours we have a boat drill. The emergency whistle (hooter) is blown and all personnel proceed to their stations on deck. We have boat drill every day at the same time. At 1600 the moorings are unfastened and the tugs start towing us out through the bay. Every one is at the portholes for their last look at the good old U.S.A. At dusk we got our first taste of blackout regulations.

===

JANUARY 9
NOTHING TO DO ON BOARD EXCEPT SLEEP AND TAKE SALT SHOWERS. AT 1100 HOURS EACH DAY WE HAVE BOAT DRILL FOR ONE HOUR. MEALS EXCELLENT AND NO CHARGE EITHER.

WATCHES SET UP ONE HOUR AT MID NITE [sic]

From the diary of Lt. Phil Darby:

I eat on the second sitting Table 16. Our waiters' name is Bernard. He's trying to get Harvey and I fat. British scones are no substitute for Amer[ican] biscuits. I am reading "Leave Her to Heaven". It's a wonderful book. I believe Ben Ames Williams wrote it.

From the diary of Lt. Paul Katz:

Just routine. Nothing Eventful [sic].

[A single entry dated Jan 9, 10, 11, 12, 13, 14 – grh]

===

JANUARY 10
SAME AS THE 9TH. LOST ANOTHER HOUR IN TIME.

From the diary of Lt. Phil Darby:

Every day we have boat drill. today [sic] for dinner we have Kippered Herring. The English love it for tea. I listened to the swing band which has been organized by the Spec[ial] Services Officer. They are serving warm Pepsi-Cola in the Officers Lounge. I'll just smoke another Webster cigar and read my book. Took a shower in salt water. It burns the lips and will not lather with regular soap.

===

JANUARY 11
SET WATCHES UP ONE HOUR. ALL THE REST ROUTINE.

From the diary of Lt. Phil Darby:

Our Steward is a narrow-minded sort of fellow. He criticizes the U.S. at every turn. Also he thinks we need instructions on being neat and orderly. We are taking the southern route.

===

JANUARY 12
SEE 11TH JAN.

From the diary of Lt. Phil Darby:

Capote of Figs and "Force" (oatmeal) for breakfast. Leavenworth and I take a stroll on the promenade deck. Sea Gulls follow the ship the entire crossing. They eat the garbage thrown off the stern. It also attracts sharks and scavengers of the sea. Gun practice forces us to go below. We have no other choice. A man overboard is a man lost. "Gentleman Jim" with Errol Flynn [sic] was shown in "C" Deck Mess Hall. We are approaching sub waters so blackout restrictions are enforced strictly. The sea is smooth, but she's listing to starboard. Must be faulty loading.

===

JANUARY 13
SEE 12TH JAN.

From the diary of Lt. Phil Darby:

There are 10,000 Infantry men in the "Salt Mines" (below water line). They're about 19 yrs average age. A tough Colonel is in charge, who continuously imposes on Air Corp personnel. Got some air on the sun deck, but the wind must be 40 mph and rain is falling. I emerged from the sack at 2:00 in the afternoon.

===

JANUARY 14
SAME ROUTINE BUT WATCHES NO CHANGE.

From the diary of Lt. Phil Darby:

Major Brown, our troop Commander, is taking dollar bills in a lottery for a guess at dock time (anchor down) in destination. I'll throw a dollar away on 0032, the 15th. A crap game has raged all day in the latrine. Naturally I rolled my usual compliment of "box cars" and "snake eyes". Darby, haven't you learned your lesson yet? My mustache is coming into its' own. I look like a bologna peddler, but it will shape up. The toilet bowls have a strange way of bubbling and getting you thoroughly soaked.

==

JANUARY 15
NEARING ENGLAND.

A BIT OF EXCITEMENT LAST NITE [sic]. A OIL TANKER TORPEDODED[sic] BY GERMAN SUBMARINES. AND SUNK. TWO MEN WERE SAVED. AIR CRAFT CARRIER (BRITISH) ALSO WAS HIT. NO DAMAGE TO OUR SHIP. WE HAVE AN ESCORT ON INTO THE UNITED KINGDOM. THE RAF GAVE OUR SHIP A GOOD BUZZ JOB.

From the diary of Lt. Phil Darby:

We have picked up a destroyer escort (two Brit. vessels). They are about a 1,000 yards on either side. Early this A.M. the ship responded to hard left rudder. A tanker was torpedoed 20 minutes off our course. I was awake when she banked sharply. Don't mind saying I was a little concerned. The Isle of Man has been sighted and we're going up the Firth of Clyde. The countryside is very green. An Aircraft Carrier catches a torpedo not ten miles from here. It's a CVE and of Independence class. The F6F's and Barracuda's which have been circling us leave as do the destroyers and go to the Carrier's side. We enter the mouth of the Clyde River. The pilot boat brings the pilot aboard. He's a dapper fellow wearing a tan jacket and green muffler. "Leabo" and I have stood at the base of the No. 2 stack for two hours. It's warm there. A submarine (P31) surfaced off the port side and can't seem to keep pace with our ship. We weigh anchor in the Port of Currock, Scotland. The Queen Elizabeth is here too. What a gigantic thing she is! We are going to disembark day after tomorrow. The port commander gave a welcome speech over the P.A. Group Capt. Bond welcomed the AAF personnel. He was apologetic for the welcome, explaining about war weary Europe, etc.

From the diary of Lt. Paul Katz:

The ship's navig[a]tor says that we are pretty close to the coast of Scotland. About 1400 we hear a lot of airplanes flying outside. I went up on deck and there were American and British carrier based planes giving us a welcome. Their carrier was about three miles away. They buzzed us for about a half hour. As we stood there watching, a puff of smoke went up from the carrier. It had been torpedoed and sunk within our sight. Twenty minutes later, a tanker in our vicinity was also sunk with the loss of 50 of the 52 crew members aboard. We learned later that there was a wolf pack of ten German submarines in that area. We reached our port later in the afternoon. I did mot get the name, but it was near Glaskow [sic].

===

JANUARY 16
DOCKED AT GUROCK, SCOTLAND AT 1600 HOURS.

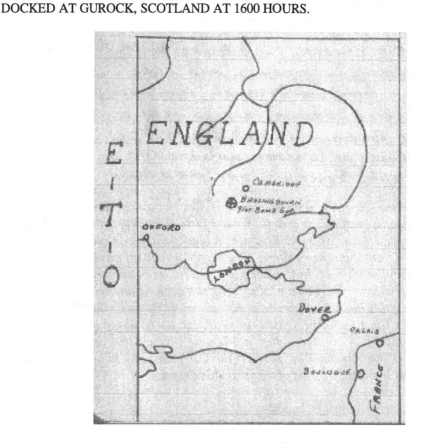

[Hand-drawn sketch of England, channel and coast of France. Metropolitan London, Dover, Oxford, Cambridge and Bassingbourn with 91st Bomb Grp identified in England; Calais and Boulogue in France - grh]

From the diary of Lt. Phil Darby:

There isn't much to do now but wait. A poker game has been going all day. It almost feels strange to walk around the ship without a life jacket. The noticeable action is the removal of cargo and luggage from the hold.

From the diary of Lt. Paul Katz:

Still aboard ship. They disembarked all the infantrymen today. Nothing eventful has happened.

===

JANUARY 17
WE WERE FERRIED ASHORE AND ON TO THE TRAINS. MY FIRST RIDE IN A BRITISH TRAIN. FILM LAND DOES NOT LIE. THE TRAINS ARE REALLY LIKE YOU SEE THEM.

LUCKY ME - I DREW THE OFFICER IN CHARGE OF THE BAGGAGE DETAIL OF SHIPMENT FZ 555 EJ.

From the diary of Lt. Phil Darby:

We are going ashore at 0800. An old river boat with a big rotary paddle in the rear picks us up. I call it a scow, but actually it's clean, and it has done it's part in this thing. A British band played us into port. We moved immediately to our troop train. The trains are so miniature. They look like play things. A Red Cross worker gives us coffee and doughnuts. It is a 16 hour trip to Stone. Scotch children line up in all the stations and try to bum cigarettes and candy from us. The LSM (London, Scotland and Midlands) has put a stop to it. We are forbidden to offer them anything. There is a dirty faced red-topped laddie who canvased me. A black-haired boy rules the boys. He is showing them something. I think a mechanical pro. The Scotch people all wave from their house windows. One family waved a British flag. In Carlisle we get off for a few minutes and have coffee. A little boy is smothered with candy by the fellas. His pop is along and receives cigarettes by the package. An English girl is holding a Brunswick recording of "Down by the Old Mill Stream" (Bing Crosby). John Hinds gets an English paper. It's quite a novelty for us. At last I choked down some of my K-rations. Played a rubber with Lowell, Phinney and Geo. Price. The buses from Stone meet us at 0200. The black out is really dark. We are fed and quartered. I'm very tired. Even these British biscuits (sections of mattress) look good.

[Playing a rubber is to play a series of bridge hands - grh]

From the diary of Lt. Paul Katz:

We are alerted to go ashore today. The tender picked us up at 1100 hours. The train was in the station. More coffee and doughnuts from the British Red Cross. The doughnuts were good but they cannot make good coffee. We boarded the train and were on our way. We are headed for a replacement pool called "Stone". We got there at 0100 in the morning.

==

JANUARY 18
BEEN ON THE TRAIN MOST OF THE DAY AND FOR MESS WE EAT "K" RATIONS. ARRIVED AT STONE, ENGLAND AT 0100 HOURS. THERE WAS A LITE[sic] RAIN. FINALLY MAKE IT TO BED AT 0230 HRS. A SMALL VILLAGE OF HANLEY ABOUT 3 MILES FROM STONE.

From the diary of Lt. Phil Darby:

I needed a blow torch to get out of bed this morning. Joe, Katz, Raber and I stumbled around in the rain getting the "processing" taken care of. We are having a great time with the English currency and monetary system. Tuppence and Thuppence! Hanley and Newcastle are close but I don't think we'll get a chance to queue for either one while we're here.

From the diary of Lt. Paul Katz:

We arrived a[t] "Stone" at 0100 in the morning and were taken right to the mess hall. Later in the morning and thru [sic] the rest of the day, we processed. I also sent you a cablegram this afternoon.

==

JANUARY 19
PROCESSED AND AGAIN FILLED OUT MANY FORMS. CHANGE MY MONEY TO ENGLISH. BARRACKS HERE ARE CALLED "BLOCKS". WE WERE QUARTERED AT HOWARD HALL BLOCK H. STILL WE HAVE NO A-3 BAGS.

From the diary of Lt. Phil Darby:

Hot Dogs! We're getting out of here. [sic] The cold and dampness is driving me nuts. It's tomorrow morning. How can I ever forget Room 32 at Stone? Reminds me of how a cell on Devils Island would be.

From the diary of Lt. Paul Katz:

Nothing to do today. We are alerted for shipment to our permanent base tomorrow.

==

JANUARY 20
LEFT STONE AT 800[sic] BY TRUCKS TO HANLEY TO TRAINS. WE ARRIVED AT ROYSTON AT
1900 HRS. TRUCKS TOOK US AND BAGGAGE TO BASSINGBOURN. FOUR CREWS WERE
ASSIGNED TO THE 91ST BOMB GROUPE.

WE WERE ASSIGNED SQUADRONS AND THEN FED. A BIG PARTY WAS IN PROCEESS.
   CREWS:
       LT. EDWARDS   TO 401ST SQD.
       LT. THOMPSON   TO 323RD SQD
       LT. BORGSTROM TO 323RD SQD
       LT. HARVEY   TO 323RD SQD
TOMMY AND MY CREW WERE ASSIGNED TO "A" BLOCK. BORGSTROM WENT TO MESS NO.2.

From the diary of Lt. Phil Darby:

*Now we know it's Bassingbourne we're headed for. That's the finest bomber base in England. We
had a long wait at the Stone station. Every part of me was numb when we boarded the train headed
for Royston. I hate to see friends getting off at all the stops. Only four crews are going to
Bassingbourne. We transferred at Cambridge. There are so many women in uniform. After we
were assigned to quarters took in a party at Mess II. What a brawl. Met the C.O. He was steeped
to the gills. Everyone really lets down their hair. I got well oiled and so did Raber. Collars and
ties were ripped off. I got into the wrong sack. Ballard was nice about it in the morning, but it isn't
the right way to start out.*

[From May 1944 to May 1945, the Commanding Officer at Bassingbourn was Col. Henry W. Terry – grh]

From the diary of Lt. Paul Katz:

*On a train again. This time we are headed for the town of Roysdon. Our field is three miles
from town. It is the pride of the Eighth Air Force. It was an old R.A.F. [Royal Air
Force - grh] field and most of the buildings are permanent. This is the field that all the big
shots land at or tour. Our barracks are pretty nice and not to[sic] cold. The food is very good as
far as overseas food goes. The British name for the field is Bassingborn[sic]. It is the home of
the 91st Bombardment Group, which is one of the original groups in England. It is located*

between Cambridge and London, about 15 miles from Cambridge and about 38 miles from London. You can judge its approximate position from the map I have drawn below.

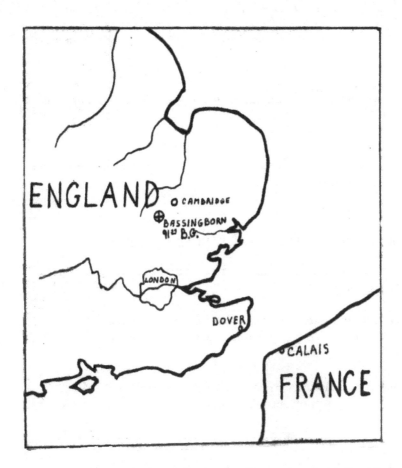

[Note his drawing is very similar to the map Lt. Harvey drew in his Jan 16 entry – grh]

==

JANUARY 21
AGAIN WE WERE PROCESSED. THIS WILL BE THE LAST TME I'M SURE. REMAINDER OF THE DAY (ALL p.m.) WAS DEVOTED TO SETTLING AND GETTING AQUAINTED.

From the diary of Lt. Phil Darby:

The weather is good here they say. Personally it is too foggy and cloudy for me. There are many navigational aides, but I can see they must all be needed. Most of the day we spent getting things settled and arranged.

From the diary of Lt. Paul Katz:

Today we started processing. Processing here doesn't consist of very much. Just filling out some new address cards and a personal history record. We also found out something about the missions and how they work. I have to fly 35 missions to complete my tour. The average time for this is six months which is why I wrote you I should be home for Thanksgiving. Some of the men in the barracks have been through 12 and more missions without ever seeing an enemy fighter or flak so the situation doesn't look to [sic] bad.

===

JANUARY 22
1ST DAY OF GROUND SCHOOL. EVEN HERE IT DOES NOT STOP.

From the diary of Lt. Phil Darby:

The boys went on a raid to Kassel - seemed to have been a milk run. The target was socked in so they bombed with PFF (or "Mickey"). Flak was very mild and erratic. We won't start flying for a week or so I imagine.

[A "milk run" is an easy mission. PFF i.e. "Path Finder Force" and "Mickey" are terms referring to the special radar targeting equipment in the radio position of some B-17's. - grh].

From the diary of Lt. Paul Katz:

Started my first day of school. I have 8 days of school before I start flying my missions.

===

JANUARY 23
2ND DAY OF SCHOOL.

From the diary of Lt. Phil Darby:

We are having ground school every day, but it isn't very tiring so I ventured into Cambridge with Bob Hodgkins. The 13 mile trip was cold as the devil in Army trucks. Ate at the Cury Cafe. Englands poverty can be noticed by the towels and bath mats for table cloths. The coffee is weak and only warm. There is no milk. Next stop was the "Criterian Pub" (public house). I have my choice between mild and bitter. The beer is naturally small in alcohol content. I drank 5 in front of the fire place (didn't even feel them). I met Ivy Clarke at the Dorothy (dance hall). They play Amer. songs "Johnsons Rag", etc. I kissed her goodnite [sic] at her "lodgings" (37 Mawsman Ave). She doesn't know anything about kissing. I want Barbara so badly. I bought Ivy a meal of "fish and chips" (shoestrings). She ate like a starved person. The English use the knife to place food on the fork. When I left, Ivy walked down Regent Street (main street). It was foggy and the giant bell tolle the hour of 12. It gave me the creeps (clop, clop, clop) walking down the street alone. Hailed a "cabby" which cost me 30 Bob (30 Shillings) to Bassingbourne.

From the diary of Lt. Paul Katz:

Second day of school.

==

JANUARY 24
3RD DAY OF SCHOOL.

From the diary of Lt. Phil Darby:

The boys were "stood down" again today. Joe Harvey and I caught the Liberty Run truck into Cambridge. "Marty" Raber instead of Joe went in with me. We ate at the Petite Cafe after the usual proceedure [sic] of getting lost. The streets are narrow, dark and winding. We again went to the Dorothy and Marty didn't dance; I only danced a couple. Met Ivy, and she learned she didn't bring the hydrogen peroxide I ordered the night before. Tonite [sic] she is dull and uninteresting. Anyhow I am glad (save pride) when she "has to be going". Marty and I headed back to camp at 2300.

From the diary of Lt. Paul Katz:

Third day of school.

==

JANUARY 25
4TH DAY OF SCHOOL.

From the diary of Lt. Phil Darby:

Not much going on. Saw "Our Hearts Were Young and Gay" on the post. Not bad - the second time for me though. Played some bridge and had a Pepsi-Cola at the Red Cross Aero Club.

From the diary of Lt. Paul Katz:

Fourth day of school.

===

JANUARY 26
5TH DAY OF SCHOOL.

From the diary of Lt. Phil Darby:

Ground School again today. The 323rd bombed a marshalling yards. Not much talk in the barracks. Must've been uneventful.

From the diary of Lt. Paul Katz:

Fifth day of school.

===

JANUARY 27
6TH DAY OF SCHOOL.
WENT TO ROYSTON IN EVENING TO A DANCE AND A PUB. BOTH WERE VERY BOREING[sic].

From the diary of Lt. Phil Darby:

We spent most of the day around the barracks and I finally got a haircut. The Limy barber accused me of taking violin lessons.

From the diary of Lt. Paul Katz:

Sixth day of school. Learned how to use the British Gee Box. It is a navigational aid using the principle of radar. It is very good and easy to learn. It is similar to the U.S. Loran.

[Both LORAN and RADAR are relatively new technologies in World War II. LORAN (long range navigation) was developed in the early 30's and used signals from radio beacons to determine a planes location. RADAR was an early 1940's development and basically still experimental at the start of the war. An early installation on Hawaii actually had detected the incoming Japanese airplanes, but the information was dismissed as the flight of un-armed B-17's being ferried over from the mainland. – grh]

==

JANUARY 28
DAY OF REST (?).   [January 28, 1945 was a Sunday. – grh]
WENT TO PICTURES IN EVENING.

From the diary of Lt. Phil Darby:

It's Royston tonight. Joe and I. A quaint little hamlet of 4,000 souls three miles away. We shopped for half an hour (the stores and shops are almost barren). I purchased a card bearing King George's picture and one of "Winny" in a cockpit. We saw "South Riding", a British production at the cinema. Was a dull show about a small town's fight for a housing project. We spent an hour in the pub at the Bull Hotel. We met two WREN's (Radar Operators) and chatted with them for a while. Danced at the Court House long enough to get bored stiff. Joe couldn't find the nerve to dance. Two pints of Scotch were raffled off. No we didn't win. We bought two packs of chips on way home.

["Winny" refers to Winston Churchill and "WREN" the Women's Royal Naval Service – grh]

From the diary of Lt. Paul Katz:

Sunday, no school today. Just lounge around camp and take it easy. Did some work on model airplane.

==

JANUARY 29
SCHOOL AGAIN. WROTE LETTERS. WORKED ON MODEL AIRPLANE (F6F).

[This was a popular pastime for the GI's. My father once related a story of several men getting into an argument about some detail on a fighter airplane one day. As typical of England, it was raining quite heavily, but to settle the argument, they all went out to where one was parked on the far end of the field to see for themselves who was correct. – grh]

From the diary of Lt. Phil Darby:

I haven't been doing any flying since arriving n England. Life seems to be moving very slowly. Nothing to do. It's driving me mad. I know there is so much to be endured. Life will soon become active. Maybe if I knew what was in store for me, I wouldn't be so anxious.

From the diary of Lt. Paul Katz:

Seventh day of school.

===

JANUARY 30
LAST DAY OF SCHOOL.
WENT TO CAMBRIDGE IN EVENING.

From the diary of Lt. Phil Darby:

Stayed on the base all day. Had a few beers at the club and didn't do much constructively.

From the diary of Lt. Paul Katz:

Eight and last day of school.

===

JANUARY 31
RETURNED TO SQUADRON FOR OPERATIONS. TOOK OUT SUBSCRIPTION TO "YANK" AND "STARS AND STRIPES". COST OF BOTH WAS 2/6 (50 cents)

MADE MY FIRST FLIGHT IN ENGLAND. INSTRUMENT CHECK WITH MAJ. TAYLOR   SQD. COMMANDING OFFICER.

MEMORANDA
MY CREW:

DARBY, PHIL N.	2ND LT.	LINCOLN, NEB	C.P. [co-pilot]
KATZ, PAUL	2ND LT.	NEW YORK CITY	NAV.
RABER, MARTIN J.	2ND LT.	NEW YORK CITY	BOMB.
JORGENSON, NEIL C.	S/SGT.	SALT LAKE CITY, UTAH	ENG. [engineer]
LLOYD, MILTON H.	S/SGT.	OMAHA, NEB	RADIO
KUS, ELMER N.	S/SGT.	CHICAGO, ILL.	WAIST G.
ODENWALLER, GEORGE H.	S/SGT.	NEW JERSEY	G (B.T)
LIMBERGER, WALTER M.	S/SGT.	HARTFORD, CONN	G (TAIL)

[This is the crew list from which I was able to locate all 9 crew members or their families. George has told me that in the initial crew assignments, he was to be the tail gunner and Walter Limberger the ball turret gunner. However, when they met they could see that the ball would be too cramped for Lindy so they traded positions. Such swaps were not uncommon making the ball turret gunner typically the smallest man on the crew. – grh]

From the diary of Lt. Phil Darby:

A flight in Ushers Able. I went along as an observer more or less. Didn't get my hands on the controls anyway.

[Per Plane Names & Fancy Noses, Pg 15, after 1942 each squadron of the 91st was assigned a two-letter code. This code was then painted in yellow on both sides of each aircraft. The 323rd Squadron was assigned the letters "OR". Each aircraft in the squadron is then assigned an additional letter. The combined designation is the radio identification of the aircraft. Per conversations with Phil Darby, "Users Able" refers to the aircraft designated by the letters OR-A on the side of the fuselage just in front of the tail section. The letters "OR" where given the phonetic of "Ushers" and the "A" is able. Per The Ragged Irregulars of Bassingbourn, Pg 224, at this time of the war OR-A identified aircraft 338939, "Peace or Bust". This aircraft failed to return and landed in France Feb 3, 1945. The 91st Bomb Group designation was the red triangle A.

Phil and George both told me that while the men had trained together as a crew, anyone could be voted off the crew if the others felt they were a problem. By this time Lt. Harvey had already had several "Regular Army" years in tanks and had been promoted to First Lieutenant in October 1942. George said that "being trained in the 'Yes Sir! – No Sir!' ways of the infantry left much to be desired with the rest of the crew including the other officers" and so they decided to vote him off the crew the next morning. However, S/Sgt. Jorgenson beat Joe to a pub that night and perhaps due to his head start at the bar, publicly informed Lt. Harvey of the feelings of his fellow crew members. The next morning, the first item on Lt. Harvey's crew meeting was an apology to his crew – something I know my father would have found very difficult to do. Yet, in my conversations with each of the crew members, all of them have stated that it was Lt. Harvey who brought them home both because of his skill as a pilot and his no nonsense attitude when flying. Their closeness and sincerity was still quite evident in each of their statements 50 years later. – grh]

From the diary of Lt. Paul Katz:

Have been assigned to the squadron and am ready to go on operational missions at any time.

==

FEBRUARY 1
PAY DAY. DREW 13 POUNDS 6 SHILLINGS AND 8 PENCE (L 13/6/8) OR $52 ROUGHLY.

FLEW THE BIG IRON BERD [sic] AND LOGED[sic] X (PASSENGER) TIME.

SCHEDULED FOR MISSION ON THE MORROW.

[English pounds/shillings/pence: 12-pence is a shilling and 20-shillings is a pound – grh]

From the diary of Lt. Phil Darby:

I had a date with Dorothea. Met her at the Lion Hotel. She brought Irene with her. I introduced her to Geo. Odenwaller (our ball turret gunner) and gave her a pass to the dance. Dottie and I went to the cinema. She is such a small thing. I find myself moderately interested in her. She is very eager, which I abhor in a woman. She walked me back to the trucks. All along the narrow streets you can see drunken GI's urinating. That is a strong influence on the English peoples opinion of us.

From the diary of Lt. Paul Katz:

No mission yet. Got paid today, but still no flying pay as I have not flown since Biggs Field.

==

FEBRUARY 2
BRIEFING AT 5:00. BREAKFAST AT 0400. OFF TO BERLIN, GERMANY.

MISSION SCRUBBED DUE TO BAD WEATHER. SCRUBBE #1 [sic].

WENT TO CAMBRIDGE IN EVENING.

ON MISSIONS WE GET A PACKAGE OF GUM AND A CANDY BAR.

From the diary of Lt. Phil Darby:

There was a Canadian USO troupe here last nite [sic]. A comedian was very good in his boy scout uniform and playing his cello. Two boys from Brooklyn did an exceptional acrobatic stunt with a jumping rope. The mistress of Ceremonies was excess baggage. Two girls singing harmony would've been better with passable acoustics. The girl who sang was marvelous. "Cheri Beri Ben" and some other classical and popular selections along with her lithe figure, beauty and poise made her the outstanding performer. She is so much like Barbara. It's startling.

From the diary of Lt. Paul Katz:

No mission yet. Had a little ground school today and that was all. One thing about this place is we are not over worked.

==

FEBRUARY 3
AGAIN TODAY I LOGGED "X" TIME ON A BLUE BOMB MISSION.

AGAIN I WENT TO CAMBRIDGE IN EVENING.

[Two notes explain this entry: The Mechanic's Note Book B-17-F Airplane, issued by the Army Air Forces Pilot School, states that an "X" should be entered in the aircraft log to indicate a major defect or unsatisfactory condition. This symbol grounds the airplane until the defect is corrected. Second is that practice bombs were painted blue. Thus, Lt. Harvey indicates he is still not on active flight status but flew a training bombing "mission". – grh]

From the diary of Lt. Phil Darby:

Mary and I saw a show in Cambridge. Walked down past the University and into the Red Cross. We had time for a cup of coffee and some doughnuts before starting back. We saw "Irish Eyes are Smiling" with June Haver. It was a very entertaining show in Technicolor.

From the diary of Lt. Paul Katz:

Nothing new today. My name is on the list for the mission tomorrow, but the squadron is "stood down", which means there will not be a mission.

==

FEBRUARY 4
FLEW PRACTICE FORMATION - WAS CO-PILOT FOR LT. HOLLIDAY. FIRST FORMATION FLYING SINCE LEAVING STATES.

From the diary of Lt. Phil Darby:

I have done so little today, I wonder if I should be paid this month. Yesterday the boys went to Big B. [Berlin - grh] The lead ship had its tail shot off. Col. Lord a fine blonde headed fella went down. Four chutes were seen. That's out of 11 men.

[Col. Lord may have been flying as a passenger as the B-17 carried a crew of 10-men when 2-waist gunners were assigned. – grh]

From the diary of Lt. Paul Katz:

No mission today due to the squadron stand down. Went up for three hours of practice flying today. This is the first time I have been off the ground since I left Biggs Filed. Navigation is very easy over England. The Gee Box makes things very easy. Today's flight was the first one that I actually knew our position every minute of the time. It was all due to the Gee Box. My name is on the list for a mission tomorrow. It will be my first one and I don't mind admitting that I am scared stiff. I am really going to pray tonight.

[Typically with four squadrons, your squadron would fly 3 missions and "stand down" the forth. – grh]

25

===

FEBRUARY 5
BREAKFAST AT 415, BRIEFING AT 515, OFF TO MUNICH, GERMANY. MISSION SCRUBBED
DUE TO WEATHER
SCRUBB NO 2.

PRACTICE FORMATION IN P.M.

ATTENDED PICTURES IN EVENING. "TALL IN THE SADDLE"

FLEW WITH LT. ADAMS.

From the diary of Lt. Phil Darby:

Mission Scrubbed

From the diary of Lt. Paul Katz:

No mission today. I was all set for it. Went to briefing and went out to the plane. We had the engines already started when the mission was scrubbed because of bad weather. However, the new list is up and I am up again for the mission tomorrow. I flew a practice mission this afternoon and have enough time to collect my back flying pay which I am going to do tomorrow.

From the diary of S/Sgt Niel Jorgenson:

First Mission

Place - Mersburg

Flak - Moderate, fairly accurate
Fighters - None   51's Escort [P-51 Fighter escort]

Damage - 3 small holes

Troubles Encountered - None

Ships Name - "Wicked Witch"

[The individual crew members are all flying as part of other crews to gain experience. See February 10 for their first mission as a crew. – grh]

FEBRUARY 6
BREAKFAST AT 400. BRIEFING AT 500. OFF TO GOTHA, GERMANY.

MISSION WAS 8 HOURS LONG. HEAVY CLOUDS WITH INSTRUMENT LET-DOWN. CEILING 400' ON LANDING. FLAK WAS LITE[sic] AND ACCURATE.

MISSION #1 COMPLETE.

AT INTERROGATION WE GET 2 OZ. OF WHISKEY!

THIS MISSION FLOWN WITH LT. ADAMS.

[It appears that flight "training" has now begun with Lt. Harvey apparently flying as co-pilot for Lt. Adams. While Lt. Darby and Lt. Katz also mention missions, they are apparently part of other crews. - grh]

From the diary of Lt. Phil Darby:

Mission Scrubbed

From the diary of Lt. Paul Katz:

Well, today was the day. Got up at 0330. Went to breakfast and then to the briefing room. The mission was on the board. There were three plans. The first, to Berlin. The second, to Mersberg and the third to a town east of Mersberg. We were briefed on all three, but all but the Mersburg raid scrubbed before we left. Went out to the plane and got ready to take off. We carried ten - five hundred pound general purpose demolition bombs. The weather was pretty bad as it generally is over England. We left the base at 0852. Flew north to Holland. When we hit the Zuyder Zee, someone yelled "flak" and I dropped everything and grabbed for my flak suit. I didn't see any of it, but it was there. We kept on going into Germany. Didn't see any fighters on the whole trip. Our target was clouded over so we didn't bomb it. On the way back, we spotted a town below us and away went the bombs. As they say, our specialty is churches, orphanages, and convents. That's about the way we did it. As long as there is a town, we will bomb it, military objectives or not. We started for home then and got some more flak. This time I could see it. There wasn't much of it, but what there was was accurate. The toggelier up in the nose got a piece of it in his chest, but he had his flak suit on and it didn't hurt him. When we got back to the base, it was closed in and we had to land in a cloud. Made it o.k. though and everything is fine with mission no. 1 behind me.

NEWSPAPER CLIPPING
(source unknown):

1,300 Heavies Strike German Industry, Rails

Heavy bombers of the 8th Air Force slashed at Germany yesterday for the first time since Saturday's record blow on Berlin as over 1,300 Fortresses and Liberators, defended by some 850 Mustangs and Thunderbolts, attacked industrial targets in the center of the Reich, mainly in the Magdeburg, Leipzig and Chemnitz areas.

Two Mustang fighter groups, the 4th and the 55th, peeled off in sectors near Leipzig and Frankfurt-on-Main to shoot up rail targets and air fields. Between them they got 29 locomotives, 37 freight cars and three planes.

Pilots of the 55th riddled a Nazi troop train, sent frantic Jerries streaming out of windows and doors and left the locomotive and cars smoking. The 4th blew up an ammunition train, pouncing on it with a hail of bullets that set off an explosion in one car and touched off another 14 box cars filled with explosives.

The RAF, too was busy during Monday night and yesterday morning, with squadrons of speedy Mosquitoes stinging Berlin and rails and communications in northwest Germany. Wellingtons of Coastal Command ranged over the Dutch coast in bad weather to slam E-boat pens along the coast.

Meanwhile, reports filtered in from neutral capitals, according to Reuter, picturing Berlin fires still smoldering after Saturday's great raid, with time bombs exploding and rescue squads wearing gas masks in some district to combat the thick smoke. Many of the bombs cascaded on the center of the city smashed water mains, making firemen helpless against flames.

End of clipping

FEBRUARY 7
BREAKFAST AT 4:15. BRIEFING AT 515. OFF TO RHUR VALLY (HAPPY VALLY) [sic] IN
GERMANY. ONLY 20 MINUTES FROM TARGET AND MISSION WAS RECALLED. HEAVY
WEATHER ALL THE WAY. INSTRUMENT LET DOWN. SCRUBB NO. 3.

SHOW IN EVENING "LAURA"

TO FLY WITH LT. HOFFMAN.

From the diary of Lt. Phil Darby:

Mission Scrubbed at Engines time.

From the diary of Lt. Paul Katz:

*Taking it easy today after yesterday's mission. Went in and drew my flying pay. Am waiting
until the 11 when the Army will send it home for me. My name is up for tomorrow's mission so
I am going to bed early. As I said the other day, I am scared as hell again. I have really
started praying every night since I got here. This is all for now, more tomorrow.*

FEBRUARY 8
BREAKFAST AT 3:30 BRIEFING AT 4:30. OFF TO WESSEL, GERMANY.
MISSION SCRUBBED DUE TO WEATHER. SCRUBB #4

LOGED [sic] LOTS OF ACTUAL INSTRUMENT TIME TODAY. INSTRUMENT LET DOWN.

TO FLY WITH LT. HOFFMAN.

From the diary of Lt. Phil Darby:

Status cancelled on account of weather.

From the diary of Lt. Paul Katz:

Got up for the mission this morning. Went to briefing & then out to the plane. Took off and started assembling over the field. The weather was so bad though, that we had to come down and land. The mission was scrubbed.

[After take-off, each B-17 would join a growing formation led by a very brightly painted B-17. Once all the aircraft have assembled, the "form-up" aircraft would depart, and the completed formation would head out over the English Channel on their mission. – grh]

FEBRUARY 9
BREAKFAST AT 530. BRIEFING AT 640. OFF TO ALTENBEKEN, GERMANY. MISSION 7-1/2 HOURS LONG. PERFECT MISSION. CLEAR DAY. DAY LITE[sic] TAKE OFF. UNDER CAST OVER TARGET. CLEAR ON LANDING. NO FLAK AND NO FIGHTERS.

MISSION #2 COMPLETE.

FLEW WITH LT. THEIS.

From the diary of Lt. Phil Darby:

Mission Scrubbed

From the diary of Lt. Paul Katz:

Not flying today as the Pilot I had yesterday is grounded with a cold. Joe is up though. Haven't flown as a complete crew yet. They usually give each man two missions with an experienced crew first.

FEBRUARY 10
BREAKFAST AT 630. BRIEFING AT 730. OFF TO KASSEL, GERMANY.

MISSION SCRUBBED DUE TO WEATHER. SCRUBB #5.

FIRST MISSION TO BE FLOWN AS A CREW. SHIPS NAME "OUT HOUSE MOUSE".
SQD [squadron – grh] IDENTIFICATION "OR N" (USSERS N-NAN). ARMY SERIAL NO. 636.

IN P.M. FLEW PRACTICE MISSION FOR 2 HOURS.

EVENING WAS SPENT AT PICTURES - "WHEN STRANGERS MARRY".

[The full aircraft designation number is 42-31636. Per information from, The Ragged Irregulars of Bassingbourn, by Marion H. Havelaar, Schiffer Publishing Ltd. 1995. The "42" indicates the contract year for the construction of the aircraft and the "31636" is the air frames unique serial number. For the planes tail number, 231636, the leading digit (4) was dropped. Documentation, especially at the squadron and group levels usually used only the last 3-digits.

The origin of the ships name is unknown but likely a result of a figure of speech used by the mother of the Operations Officer, William Reid. While the crew diary's generally show the name as "Out House Mouse" (probably because of the slanted "T" in the name on the nose art), the name appears as "Outhouse Mouse" in most reference books that I've seen. In any case, the tail number clearly identifies it as the same aircraft.

Additional comments may be found after the February 12th entry by Lt. Katz and in the aircrafts brief history near the end of this book. – grh]

From the diary of Lt. Phil Darby:

Mission Scrubbed. I visited Cambridge again.

From the diary of Lt. Marty Raber:

Primary Tank Factory
Secondary RR Yards Castle
Stations 0900
Engines 9:30
Taxi   9:40
Takeoff 1000
Depart Base 1136

Scrubbed

[This is the first entry on the first page of Lt. Raber's diary. He did not give a date, but it does appear to be the same as Lt. Harvey's mission so I have placed it here. – grh]

From the diary of Lt. Paul Katz:

I was up for a mission today, but the weather was bad so the mission was scrubbed. The next time we fly, it will be with our complete crew.

==

FEBRUARY 11
BREAKFAST AT 305. BRIEFING AT 405. OFF TO MUNSTEN, GERMANY.

MISSION SCRUBBED DUE TO WEATHER. SCRUBB #6.

PICTURES IN EVENING "ONE BODY TOO MANY".

From the diary of Lt. Phil Darby:

Mission Scrubbed after Engines started.

From the diary of Lt. Marty Raber:

Target RR Yards Munsing

[This is the second page of Lt. Raber's diary and is also undated. – grh]

From the diary of Lt. Paul Katz:

Up for a mission again today, but the weather is still bad. No flying again.

===

FEBRUARY 12
NO FLYING DUE TO BAD WEATHER.

RATHER QUIET DAY ALL AROUND.

From the diary of Lt. Phil Darby:

Mission was recalled just as we reached the Channel. Tons of bombs were dumped in the Channel at Point-A.

[For the safety of the airbase and its rescue personnel, the aircraft and its aircrew, the bombers were not to land with live bombs on board. – grh]

From the diary of Lt. Paul Katz:

No mission again today due to the weather. We have our own ship assigned to us now. It is called "Outhouse Mouse" and has a picture of a mouse standing in the open door of an outhouse. It is an old ship and has had quite a few missions. It is a good ship though and has a steel reinforced floor in the nose which I like. It helps keep the flak out.

[Lt. Katz's seated navigator position in a B-17 is on the left side of the aircraft and behind the bombardier (or the toggelier when Marty Raber was flying lead bombardier) whose position is in the Plexiglas nose. The seated cockpit positions of the pilot, on the left side of the aircraft and co-pilot (Phil Darby) on the right side are above and behind them. The flight engineer (Niel Jorgenson) is behind and between the pilot and co-pilot where he can monitor all the critical gauges and the health of the aircraft throughout the mission. He also serves as the top-turret gunner. Behind him, is the bomb bay, then the ball-turret gunner (George Odenwaller) whose position is accessed through a small door that opens through the floor of the aircraft when the Plexiglas ball is rotated straight down. In the narrowing waist on the left side of the aircraft is the radioman (Milton Lloyd). Behind him, the one waist gunner on this crew (Al Kus). Al often flew as a "radar jammer". Al said that there were only three B-17's in the squadron equipped with the special jamming equipment but they were essential to the safety of the squadron as they interfered with the radar aiming systems of the German flak gunners. Flak actually caused more damage than the fighters. Supported by a bicycle style seat when knelling on his knees in the very tail of the "Out House Mouse" was the tail gunner (Walter Limberger). This was Lt. Harvey's assigned crew and their positions aboard the "Out House Mouse".

As Paul has stated, this was an "old" airplane that had already seen several aircrews. George Odenwaller told me that because it was still dark when they were taken out to their aircraft at the start of a mission, it was only after the mission that the crew was able to walk around and inspect their assigned B-17. The "Out House Mouse" was painted in the earlier flat green, brown and gray camouflage paint scheme and had numerous patches covering flak damage of earlier missions. When they were heard lamenting their fate in drawing an old, ugly war-horse instead of one of the shiny new replacement airplanes, one of the ground-crew informed them "they were lucky to draw that aircraft because she would bring you home".

An early G model, the "Out House Mouse" retained the "cheek" guns on either side of the nose despite the new addition of the "chin turret" under the nose. The chin turret was operated by the bombardier. Initially without any nose armament, the German fighter pilots quickly realized that the B-17 was most vulnerable to a direct frontal attack when the fighter was between the lower travel of the upper turret and the upper travel of the ball turret. During the course of the war, several solutions to this unprotected space had been tried. One earlier solution was the "cheek guns" that can be seen on the "Out House Mouse" just above the nose art in the photograph section of the book. The ultimate solution however, seemed to be the twin 0.50cal, remote controlled chin turret that came standard on all the B-17G models. The chin turret alone was later proven to still be inadequate so the cheek guns were again added on the final B-17G configuration. Later G models also included staggered waist gun positions, used lighter metal in their airframes and were left unpainted to reduce the weight of the tough B-17 and extend its maximum range just a little more. Perhaps because the "Out House Mouse" predates these later changes, she was better able to survive the damage of a mission and safely return her crew home. As noted later, the "Out House Mouse" attained the second best combat reliability record of the entire 8th Air Force – 139 missions without an abort. The "Out House Mouse" and her ground crew took very good care of my father and his aircrew. – grh]

===

FEBRUARY 13
BREAKFAST AT 330. BRIEFING AT 430. OFF TO DRESDEN, GERMANY.

MISSION SCRUBBED DUE TO WEATHER. SCRUBB #7.

WENT TO CAMBRIDGE IN EVENING.

From the diary of Lt. Phil Darby:

Mission Scrubbed. Not much doing.

From the diary of Lt. Paul Katz:

No mission today. Weather again. Raber was in the hospital for two days. He is out now, but will not fly with us tomorrow due to the tail end of a cold. We are [up] for a mission tomorrow. The sky is clear tonight and the stars are out. That doesn't mean anything though as the weather is very changeable here.

FEBRUARY 14
BREAKFAST AT 330. BRIEFING AT 430. OFF TO DRESDEN, GERMANY.
CLEAR DAY. FLEW MY OWN SHIP, "OUT HOUSE MOUSE". TWO SQUADRONS RUN TOGETHER ON ROUTE. WE WERE THROWN OUT OF FORMATION. LOST #4 ENGINE TRYING TO CATCH FORMATION. WE HAD TO COME HOME ALONE ON 3 ENGINES AT 135 I.A.S. FROM 150 MILES IN GERMANY. GOT FLAK JUST BEFORE ENTERING FRANCE. WE SALVOED [released - grh] BOMBS AND DID NOT FOLLOW BOMBER STREAM HOME. EVERYONE FRIGHTENED BUT WITH GOOD NAVIGATION AND HARDWORK OF CREW, WE MADE IT. IT IS A WONDER WE MADE IT SINCE WE CUT THRU [sic] ONE EDGE OF RHUR VALLY [sic]. GROUPE BOMBED PRAGUE, CHECZ. [sic] AND SCATTERED OVER FRANCE AND BELGIUM OUT OF GAS. LOTS OF BATTLE DAMAGE TOO. MISSION QUITE ROUGH DUE TO POOR LEADERSHIP. 7-1/2 HRS. LENGTH.

MISSION #3 COMPLETE.

[Even today Dresden remains a controversial target as the city was known for its art and culture and had little military significance. However, since Germany had now been bombing civilian London for nearly 5 years and because the Allies were still unsuccessful in getting Germany to discuss surrender, Dresden had been placed on the target list in February 1945 due to its communications and railway facilities. It was attacked again on April 17th and by the end of the war, Dresden had been reduced to a wasteland of rubble. Because of the sensitivity of targeting Dresden, Phil Darby told me that the brass really gave the "Out House Mouse" a close inspection when it returned to base to be sure that the crew really did have mechanical problems and had not aborted for some other reason.

Without the covering gun support provided by the close B-17 formation, a lone and damaged B-17 was an easy and much sought after target for the German fighter pilots and one they would always attack. For their first completed mission as a crew, it was no doubt a very frightening and seemingly endless return trip home through miles of enemy territory. As Paul states in his diary which follows, only 7 of 36 planes made it back to base. Per Phil Darby, "135 I.A.S." refers to Indicated Air Speed. With a cruising speed of 160 m.p.h. when fully loaded with bombs and fuel, the now wounded but empty "Out House Mouse" was going to take over an hour just to get out of Germany. - grh]

From the diary of Lt. Phil Darby:

Mission #1
We aborted near Munster on the way to Dresden. Lost one engine, salvoed bombs and returned thru[sic] the Ruhr. We caught 5 bursts off left wing on our route. Went too close to Essen. What

an experience for first mission. We were knocked out of formation by another squadron trying to get out of flak area.

From the diary of Lt. Paul Katz:

Today was the day. I don't think I was ever closer to death than I was today. Thank God we got back alright. Our mission was to bomb Dresden. The weather was fine which is bad for us as the anti-aircraft gunners can see us and shoot at us visually. We flew out over the North Sea and hit flak as soon as we crossed the Zuider Zee. It wasn't two[sic] bad there. Then we headed down into Germany. The Flak really started coming up. It was accurate. About that time, 100 miles from target, our formation broke up. Another squadron trying to avoid Flak ran through us and we were all over the sky. We tried to get back into the formation and lost[the] #4 engine. Well, that settled matters. We couldn't keep up with the group on three engines. We had to go back thru[sic] the most heavily defended area of Germany alone. From here on in, it was up to me. I don't think I ever worked as hard with a pencil and paper as I did today. Our shortest route home was over the Rhur Valley, which has more Flak guns than the rest of the enemy put together. We made our turn and I gave Joe a heading to fly. I don't know what the rest of the crew was doing, but I was praying like I never prayed before. I could see your face in front of me and I was saying good-bye to you. I didn't expect to make it back. There was one corridor five miles wide that didn't have any Flak. It was[up] to me to get us down that lane. God must have been with me, we just made the southern tip of it. We got a little Flak, but no one was hurt. From[there] I headed for Belgium and then home. Seven ships out of thirty-six returned to the field. The others had to land in France and on the continent. Six ships are still unaccounted for. I am going to town tonight and get drunk. I didn't after the first mission, but after today, we need it. I got a big kick out of one of the gunners after we landed. He got out of the ship and poked his head in the nose. "Are you the navigator?" he asked. I said "Yes". He just smiled and said, "That was a good job of navigating" then left. Just to hear him say that made me feel good all over.

From the diary of S/Sgt Niel Jorgenson:

Second Mission

Place - Dresden

Flak - Heavy, accurate
Fighters - None - 51's escort

Damage - 2 small holes

Trouble Encountered - #4 engine feathered, was knocked out of formation. Came back all way alone unescorted. Burned up other three engines. Cranked BB doors & flaps [bomb bay doors & flaps are apparently inoperative. Cranking is a very tiring operation. – grh]

Ships Name - "Out House Mouse"

From the "Mission Sheet" of S/Sgt George Odenwaller:

MISSION:	*#1*
TARGET:	*DRESDEN (LEAD UNIT HIGH - LOW UNIT PRAGUE, CHECH)*
FLAK:	*MODERATE ACCURATE*
FIGHTERS:	*NONE*
DAMAGE:	*LOST No.1 ENGIN [sic] - FLAK !*
TAKE-OFF:	*7:25*
E.T.R.	*3:35*
T.T:	*8:10*
OXYGEN TIME:	*6 HOURS*
BOMB LOAD:	*8 G.P.'s & 2 CLUSTERS OF INCENDARIES*
ALT:	*27,000 FT.*
SHIP No:	*636*
NAME:	*OUTHOUSE MOUSE OR-N*
TEMP:	*- 38 F.*

MY FIRST MISSION ! SCARED STIFF - HAD TROUBLE WITH MY GUNS WHILE INSTALLING BARRELS. HAD TO ABORT AFTER REACHING THE I.P. No.1 ENGIN [sic] HIT BY FLAK - FLEW HOME ALONE ON 3 - NO FIGHTER PROTECTION.
SALVOED BOMBS
AT ABOUT THE I.P., A SILVER P-51D WITH GERMAN MARKINGS CAME RIGHT UP INTO OUR FORMATION - PILOT WAVED, PULLED UP & WAS GONE - EVERYONE WAS SO SURPRISED NOT A SHOT WAS FIRED AT THIS INTRUDER. (WAS A CAPTURED A/C)
LEARNED YEARS LATER, THIS P-51 WAS BASED AT TEMPLEHOFF AIRDROME. MOVED THEN TO DRESDEN-KLOTZCHE, 44-45.

[Abbreviations used by George:
 A/C   Aircraft
 E.T.R. Estimated Time of Return
 T.T.   Total Time
 I.P.   Initial Point [The starting point of the bomb run. From here the flight had to be straight and level until "bombs-away" regardless of the flak, fighters or any other enemy defense. During this time the aircraft is actually being flown by the bombardier using the Top Secret Nordon Bomb site - grh]
 G.P.   General Purpose
 M-17   Cluster/Fragmentation bombs
 Chaff   Silver foil - 1/8" x 10" thrown out of a/c by radioman to shut down German radar flak guns - grh]

From the diary of S/Sgt Walter Limberger:

#1

Target – Prague, Checz

Flak – Moderate

Fighters – None

Damage – None

Take Off – 07:25

Landed – 15:35

Total Time – 8 hrs 10 min

Oxygen – 6 hrs

Bombs – 8-500 G.P.'s and 2-M17's (Fire Bombs)

Altitude – 27,000 ft.

Ship # – 636 Out House Mouse

Temp – -38°

First one and it seemed sort of rough. We had to abort just after we reached the G.P. We dropped our bombs, feathered an engine and came on back alone. Also had a close call. Oxygen hose to my mask had become disconnected and nearly passed out. A flak burst damaged #3 engine therefore dropping out of formation.

[This is a good example of a discrepancy among the diaries. The engines are numbered from left to right from the perspective of the flight crew. Thus, the number one engine is the left, outboard engine and the number four is the right, outboard engine.   In any case, all agree that the damaged engine forced them out of the formation and into a long, lonely and frightening flight home. – grh]

NEWSPAPER CLIPPING - Dated Thursday February 15, 1945

8th Hits Dresden to Help Reds

Koniev Near Saxony in
2-Pronged Drive to
Split Germany

The heart of Germany rocked with tremendous explosions yesterday as more than 1,300 8th Air Force heavy bombers dropped tons of high explosives and incendiaries on transportation and industrial targets in three important cities -- including Dresden, still blazing from the effects of a double RAF blow the night before, and threatened by the advance, less than

70 miles away, of Red Army troops. Both the 8th Air Force and RAF attacks on Dresden were in support of one offensive of Marshal Koniev's forces, smashing toward the city in a bid to cut the Reich in two, while another drive struck north toward Berlin.

German "Achtung" reports last night indicated continuing air attacks over western Germany.

Heavies Plaster Arms Factories

Heavy bombers of the 8th Air Force, idle since last weekend's operations, thundered out yesterday in support of Red Army salients aimed toward the heart of Germany, when more than 1,300 Fortresses and Liberators dealt solid blows to the industrial cities of Dresden, Chemnitz and Magdeburg. They dropped heavy explosives and incendiaries.

Dresden, in the path of the Soviet offensive, and never before hit by a great weight of 8th AF bombs, was the focal point of the attack, which followed the RAF's double-barrelled blow on the city the night before. Of a force of 1,400 RAF bombers which struck oil and industrial targets in the Reich Tuesday night and yesterday morning, 800 veered off to Dresden to rock the city in two separate raids.

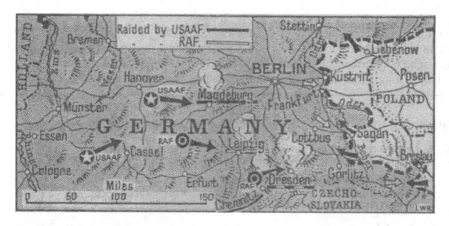

Fortresses which battered Dresden yesterday met thick clouds and had to bomb by instrument. The city, which has large railway yards and factories producing such vital war supplies as shells, rifles, machine-guns and industrial tools, has been reported to be housing thousands of evacuees from bombed-out areas, some of them even from Berlin.

Chemnitz, only 35 miles southwest of Dresden, also was pounded by Fortresses through clouds. This city has four railway yards, one large marshalling yard and railroad repair shops. Industrially, it is a machine tool and armaments center, turning out such war items as lathes, gear cutters, trucks, shells, turbines and steam engines.

Liberators in strong force concentrated on well-battered Magdeburg, which also suffered from RAF blows the night before. Two hours before the three-pronged air offensive, which took place shortly after noon, a small force of heavies attacked a six-span road bridge across the Rhine at Wesel, in the northwest corner of the Ruhr.

The bombers went out with a shield of more than 900 Mustangs and Thunderbolts, some of which carried out strafing[sic] attacks on communications targets in southwest and western Germany. Early reports last night gave the fighters 64 locomotives and 139 railway cars as their toll for the day.

Meanwhile, the 15th Air Force lent more force to the Allied air blow when Fortresses and Liberators based in Italy blasted oil targets and communications in Vienna and other formations of heavies ranged over Jugoslavia[sic] to hammer rail-yards for the second consecutive day.

Another Clipping:

Dresden 'Heap of Ruins'
Dresden -- pounded Wednesday and Thursday by the 8th, following a heavy two-wave night attack by the RAF -- was described in German reports as "a heap of ruins." The Berlin correspondent of the Stockholm Dagens Nyheter declaired that "tens of thousands," many of them refugees who had small chance to find shelter, had perished in the raids, while a Moscow report said that Dresden was now in the throes of panic, endless columns of refugees streaming into the city as others tried to leave.

Chemnitz, just 35 miles from Dresden and equally important to Nazi defenses in the east, suffered almost the same fate, according to Berlin Radio.

End of Clippings

["German 'Achtung'" is the German radio. – grh]

==

FEBRUARY 15
BREAKFAST AT 630. BRIEFING AT 730. OFF TO ESSEN, GERMANY.
LOTS OF FLAK OVER TARGET. FLEW ELEMENT LEADHOME [sic]. GOT LOTS OF FLAK HOLES
IN SHIP. LT. KATZ (NAVIGATOR) GOT FLAK HOLE IN PANTS LEG. MY WINDSHIELD BROKEN
BY FLAK. INSTRUMENT LET-DOWN UPON RETURN TO FIELD.
6-1/2 HOUR MISSION.
MISSION #4 COMPLETE.

[The diary records for February 15, 16 and 17 differ, some reporting a scrub and others reporting a mission to Essen, Lipzig or Gelsenkirchen. The Benzol plants at Gelsenkirchen are reported by Lt. Harvey's newspaper clipping pasted into his Feb. 15 entry and transcribed below.   In any case, after reading all of the records, it is clear that navigator Katz had a very close call as well as the pilot.

Flak was an exploding steel artillery shell that exploded at a present altitude sending sharp, jagged pieces of steel in all directions – the air equivalent to the hand-grenade.   The shrapnel ranged in size from marbles to small footballs and caused more damage to the bombers than anything else. The flak gunners had only to come close and then the bombers would fly into it, have it rain down on them, or have it blown into them from explosions below, behind or beside them. My father brought back 4 pieces of flak that he picked up from his cockpit floor – probably from this mission. The one piece I have is about 2-inches long by about 1-inch wide and is a little less than half an inch thick. It weighs several ounces and is still very sharp.   I am told that the windshield on the B-17 was about an inch or more thick, which provides us an idea of how forceful the flak hits could be. The position of the navigator's table is by the window located below and forward of the pilot and just aft of the nose-art on the left-hand side of the aircraft.

To provide some clarification to the diaries, the combat mission record in Appendix , page 207 of the book The Ragged Irregulars of Bassingbourn, lists the mission of Feb 14 as targeting Prague; Feb. 15 as targeting Dresden; and the mission of Feb. 16 as targeting Gelsenkirchen. All of these missions are shown as being completed. The Feb. 17 mission targeting Bohlen is shown as having been recalled and the Feb. 18 mission targeting Altenbeken, is shown as being scrubbed. – grh]

From the diary of Lt. Phil Darby:

Mission #2
Bombed Gelsenkirchen, a Bezol plant between two canals. Flak was heavy and very accurate. We had 25 holes in "Lewd Angel" when we returned.

From the diary of Lt. Marty Raber:

Target Benzoil Plant Munster
Sec RR Yards Munster

We met heavy Flak over target our plane was hit 12 times. One piece cut the navag. [ator] pants. No planes shot down. The bomb hit his[sic] target.

40

[Marty told me that hearing the flak go through the aircraft right behind him, he was afraid to look back at Katz. After calling over his shoulder and hearing that Paul was okay, he turned and saw Paul's bewildered expression as he inspected the holes in his flight suit. – grh]

From the diary of Lt. Paul Katz:

Up again today for a mission to Essen. I got a small souvenir out of this one and it is the kind I don't want to get again. We were hit by Flak over the target and got about 50 holes in the ship. One piece, which is my souvenir, came in the nose and went thru [sic] *both my pants legs. That just about scared the life out of me, when I realized how close it came. We got back alright though and everything is o.k. No casualties.*

From the diary of S/Sgt Niel Jorgenson:

Third Mission

Place - Gelsinkirchen
Flak - Heavy & accurate
Fighters - None 51's escourt

Damage - 23 holes, navigator had pant legs cut, tail and close call. Dropped two gas tanks.

Troubles encountered - None

Ships Name - "Lewd Angel"

From the "Mission Sheet" of S/Sgt George Odenwaller:

MISSION:	*#2*
TARGET:	*GELSENKIRCHEN*
FLAK:	*INTENSE & ACCURATE*
FIGHTERS:	*NONE*
DAMAGE:	*27 HOLES IN A/C*
TAKE-OFF:	*7:10*
E.T.R:	*4:50*
OXYGEN TIME:	*6 HOURS - 40 MIN*
T.T:	*9 HOURS - 40 MIN*
BOMB LOAD:	*8 500LB G.P.'s & 2 CLUSTERS*
ALT:	*26,000 FT*
SHIP No:	*755*
NAME:	*LEWED ANGEL LG-A*
TEMP:	*- 42 F.*

REALLY A ROUGH ONE. HEATED SUIT WENT OUT OVER TARGET. FLAK MISSED TAIL GUNNER's HEAD BY INCHES. NAVIGATOR's CLOTHS TORN BY FLAK. RIPPED OUT THE SEAT OF

HIS PANTS AS HE STOOD UP IN NOSE. PLANE WAS PRETTY WELL TORN UP! ACUTALLY SWEATED OVER TARGET EVEN THOUGH HEATED SUIT WAS OUT & IT WAS -42F.

From the diary of S/Sgt Walter Limberger:

#2

Target – Gelsnkirchen, Ger.

Flak – Intense

Fighters – None

Damage – 25 Holes

Take Off – 07:10

Landed – 16:50

Total Time – 9 hrs 40 min

Oxygen – 6 hrs 40 mins

Bombs – 8-500 G.P.'s 2-Incendiary Clusters

Altitude – 26,000 ft.

Ship # – 014 Lewd Angel

Temp – -42°

Pretty rough today. Got a piece of flak in my position 2 inches from my head. Plenty scared. Also, navigator nearly got it in both legs as a piece of flak went through both of his flight suit legs.

[Some discrepancy appears about the aircraft number. The Ragged Irregulars of Bassingbourn and Plane Names & Fancy Noses, both list the aircraft number of "Lewd Angel" as 338755 which agrees with S/Sgt Odenwaller's diary.

While the ground crews were thankful their aircraft had made it back from its mission, being full of flak holes no doubt drew a strong comment from the crew chief. The aircraft were actually assigned to the crew chief of the ground crew, and he had "allowed" the aircrew to use HIS air-worthy B-17 for their mission. Now with so many flak holes in the aircraft he undoubtedly informed the aircrew that he fully expected them to return HIS aircraft in the same condition it had been in when he gave it to them – especially since they were NOT the regular crew. – grh]

NEWSPAPER CLIPPING (Source unknown):
[This same clipping in Lt. Raber's scrapbook includes the date of the newspaper - Saturday, Feb. 17, 1945 – grh]

1,000 Heavies Hit Nazi Oil -
Also Pound
West Front
Rail Lines

More than 1,000 8th Air Force heavy bombers struck powerful blows to destroy the remaining one-fifth of German oil production yesterday when they bombed oil refineries and benzol plants at Dortmund, Salzbergen and Gelsenkirchen, and raised more havoc with German rail communications to the Western Front by blasting the large marshalling yards of Hamm, Osnabruck and Rheine.

Out for the third successive day of improved weather, Fortresses and Liberators, escorted by approximately 200 Mustangs, hit two oil refineries at Dortmund and Salzbergen, as well as two plants making benzol, a vital compound for manufacture of synthetic oil, in the Ruhr industrial area, near Dortmund and Gelsenkirchen.

Blasted 3rd Day in Row

Other German oil targets and rail communications in the Vienna area were blasted for the third successive day by strong forces of 15th Air Force heavy bombers, as RAF medium and heavy bombers hit an oil refinery in northern Italy.

A special target which the 15th Air Force also attacked was the Obertraubling airdrome at Regensburg, base for the new jet-propelled Me262 planes.

Bombing of oil targets by the 8th heavies was done visually. There were no reports at a late hour last night of losses or of enemy opposition to the Forts and Liberators. USSTAF announced that the losses in Thursday's raids, previously announced as 15 bombers and six fighters, had dropped to 12 bombers and two fighters. The previously - unannounced Wednesday losses were given as eight bombers and five fighters.

End of clipping

[The "new jet-propelled Me262 planes" look like conventional jet aircraft of the 1950's. – grh]
==

FEBRUARY 16
BREAKFAST AT 600. BRIEFING AT 700. OFF TO LIPZIG, GERMANY.
MISSION RECALLED DUE TO WEATHER. INSTRUMENT LET-DOWN. DUMPED BOMBS IN ENGLISH CHANNEL. EACH SHIP CARRIED 12 - 250LB GENERAL PURPOSE BOMBS AND THERE WERE AT LEAST 1000 SHIPS. WHAT A WASTE OF TIME AND MONEY.
SCRUBB #8

From the diary of Lt. Phil Darby:

Mission Scrubbed today.

From the diary of Lt. Paul Katz:

Was up for a mission again today and got as far as the channel when it was scrubbed and we dropped our bombs in the ocean. No credit for a mission so I still have three.

FEBRUARY 17

FORGOT THIS DAY TO RITE [sic] IN THIS BOOK. SQUADRON PARTY TONITE, OH, BOY!

===

FEBRUARY 18
BREAKFAST AT 300. BRIEFING AT 400. OFF TO ALTEN BEKEN, GERMANY.
MISSION SCRUBBED DUE TO WEATHER BEFORE ENGINES TIME.

48 HOUR PASS EFFECTIVE AT 1200 HOURS.

WENT TO LONDON. VERY DISAPPOINTED IN CITY. SAW PICCADILLY CIRCUS!

SCRUBB #9

From the diary of Lt. Phil Darby:

Mission scrubbed again.

Our first 48 hr pass, and off to London. Arrived in London at Kings Cross Sta[tion] and caught a cab up to Russell Square.

From the diary of Lt. Paul Katz:

Today's mission was scrubbed due to weather.
48 hour pass to London.

[Once again, Lt. Katz makes a multi-day entry. This one is dated Feb. 18, 19 and 20. – grh]

===

FEBRUARY 19
RETURNED TO CAMBRIDGE FROM LONDON. DID A BIT OF SHOPPING.

From the diary of Lt. Phil Darby:

Harvey went home to Bassingbourn, Katz and I stayed on at the Russell Hotel. Saw all the sights in London: Picadilly [sic] Sq., London Tower, #10 Downing St., Buckingham, London Bridge, Parliament, Wellington Guard House, Hyde Park, St. Paul's Cathedral, Big Ben, Waterloo Bridge, Trafalgar Square (Lions) and Westminster Abbey.

===

FEBRUARY 20
SPENT DAY IN CAMBRIDGE. WENT TO PICTURES "IN SOCIETY".

PASS ENDS AT MIDNITE [sic].

From the diary of Lt. Phil Darby:

We got up late today at the hotel. Took a run over to the Reindeer Red Cross Club. Met "Horace Morris" Lovell and his Navigator Phinney. Last night saw Quentin and Bill Emmet, Hoffman. Met Jack Charlesworth in London Officers PX.

===

FEBRUARY 21
SQUADRON STAND-DOWN. SCHOOL ALL DAY. GOT LOTS OF LETTERS FROM MY WIFE. WENT TO PICTURES IN EVENING "TO HAVE AND TO HAVE NOT". DAMNED GOOD TOO!!!

[For a normal mission, the bomber formation consisted of 3 of the 4 squadrons assigned to the group. The 91st Bomb Group had the 322, 323, 324 and 401 Bomb Squadrons. The forth Squadron "stood-down" that day. To meet the mission requirements, aircraft were "loaned" to the other participating squadrons or may have served as "spares". A "spare" aircraft would be made ready by the ground-crew, fueled and loaded with bombs and ammunition ready to be used should a committed aircraft have to abort due to a malfunction during take-off or assembly. In such instances, the crew simply changed to the "spare" aircraft and joined up with rest of the formation. An exception was a ME (maximum effort) mission where all available aircraft participate. – grh]

From the diary of Lt. Phil Darby:

45

Squadron stand down today. We sure needed the rest after that week-end in London. Saw Humphrey Bogart picture this evening.

From the diary of Lt. Paul Katz:

Squadron stand down. No mission today.

==

FEBRUARY 22
BREAKFAST AT 400. BRIEFING AT 500. OFF TO STENDAL, GERMANY.

VERY GOOD MISSION. BOMBED MARSHALLING YARDS. NO FLAK. ENCOUNTERED FIGHTERS. ONE BLEW UP IN FRONT OF OUR SHIP. THEY WERE GERMAN P51's AND JET's 262's. FIGHTERS MADE A PASS AT OUR FORMATION. ONE BOMBER DOWN BY FIGHTERS AND ONE LOST IN CHANNEL ON RETURN. A VERY GOOD MISSION. 8-1/2 HOURS LONG. BOMBED FROM 12,000 FEET.

MISSION #5 COMPLETE

[Recall that on Feb 14, S/Sgt. Odenwaller noted a P-51 with German markings. Apparently Germany is using captured allied aircraft to augment their own. – grh]

From the diary of Lt. Phil Darby:

Mission #3
Bombed marshalling yards at Stendal (50 miles west of Berlin). Beautiful navigation - no flak. Bandits [enemy fighters - grh] *did not get to us but we saw dog fights all around. ME-262 (Jet propelled) flew by. God bless the P-51 boys.*

From the diary of Lt. Marty Raber:
Target RR Yards at Stendal To Stop Tra[i]ns.
Secondary Target Any means of Transportation.

We made a visual run at 12,300FT. No Flak was encountered. We were attacked by Fighters. Saw 3 shot down. One P51 (German), Me410, Me109. Saw one Me 262. One 17 in the formation ahead was shot down. None lost in our Group.

[From his position in the Plexiglas nose of the B-17, Lt. Raber has a clear, unobstructed view ahead. S/Sgt. Limberger in the tail gets to see where they have been and S/Sgt. Odenwaller in the ball, can view 360-degrees around and down. The pilot and co-pilot actually have two of the more restricted views as the nose blocks their forward view, and the engines block their view to the sides. – grh]

From the diary of Lt. Paul Katz:

46

Rail center near Berlin today. The papers played this raid up quite a bit as we went to the target at 12,000 feet which is very low. The newspapers say we went in at 1,500 ft. but they just like to exaggerate. In spite of the low altitude, it was pretty easy. We didn't get any Flak at all. (Thank God, at that altitude, we would have been dead ducks.) The group next to us were hit by fighters, but we got off without any trouble.

From the diary of S/Sgt Niel Jorgenson:

Fourth Mission

Place - Stendal

Altitude - 12,000 feet

6,000 Alied [sic] aircraft in the raid.

Flak - Little innacurate [sic]
Fighters - German flown P-51 & Jet 262

Ships Name - "Ramblin Rebel"

"Mission Sheet" of S/Sgt George Odenwaller:

MISSION:	*#3*
TARGET:	*STENDAL*
FLAK:	*NONE*
FIGHTERS:	*ME 262's / ME163 ROCKET A/C*
DAMAGE:	*NONE*
TAKE-OFF:	*8:20*
E.T.R:	*5:25*
OXYGEN TIME:	*7 HOURS*
T.T:	*9 HOURS - 5 MIN*
BOMB LOAD:	*12 250LB G.P.'s*
ALT:	*12,000 FT*
SHIP No:	*841*
NAME:	*[None shown]*
TEMP:	*- 10 F.*

SOMETHING NEW IN BOMBING - FLEW VERY LOW TO BOMB - WENT AROUND FLAK AREAS. SAW A ME 262 WAY OUT OF RANGE - FIRST TIME I SAW AN ENEMY A/C BLOW UP AND GO DOWN. OUR P-51 FIGHTERS NAILED 26 ENEMY A/C TO-DAY [sic]. NEVER SAW SO MANY B-17's AT ONCE IN THE AIR. FIGHTER PROTECTION GOOD! SAW MY FIRST ME 163 ROCKET A/C - SPEED APPROX. 500-600 M.P.H. - COULD NOT KEEP TURRET GUNS ON IT - TOO FAST.

From the diary of S/Sgt Walter Limberger:

#3

Target – Stendel, Germany
Flak – None
Fighters – Some in area
Damage – None
Take Off – 08:20
Landed – 1725
Total Time – 9 hrs 5 min
Oxygen – 7 hrs
Bombs – 24 - 250 pounders
Altitude – 12,000 ft.
Ship # – 841 No Name
Temp – -10°

Didn't go very high today. We went around flak area. We had a few fighters jump us, but no damage – saw an ME163 Rocket powered fighter. It went so fast I could hardly track it. Our P-51 escort shot down several of the fighters.

[The Me262 is the German jet fighter that looks very similar to conventional jet fighters. The Me163 Rocket aircraft is a much smaller aircraft with a delta wing configuration. The aircraft is "launched" into the air using a platform similar to that used by the V-1 rockets. The landing gear is dropped after the launch. Flight time was very short consisting of a very rapid climb, a brief fight, followed by a rapid plunge back down to the ground. – grh]

NEWSPAPER CLIPPING - THE STARS AND STRIPES - Friday Feb. 23, 1945

2nd Biggest Blitz Hits Nazis

6,000 Planes Swoop Down to Pinpoint Rail, Canal System

The greatest mass assault since the Normandy invasion was loosed by more than 6,000 Allied aircraft yesterday against the entire system of German rail communications in Western Europe as planes from seven different commands - including heavy bombers from the 8th Air Force, the 15th Air Force, and RAF Bomber Command - dropped a tremendous weight of bombs almost simultaneously on hundreds of targets throughout western Germany and northern Holland.

In weather so clear that airmen could see for 50 miles, the Allied air forces thundered through the skies to carry out the vast, long planned operations of smashing all highways, railways, and canals connected with central Germany.

The 8th Air Force led the gigantic flying arsenal with more than 1,400 Liberators and Fortresses which, escorted by 800 Mustangs and Thunderbolts, blasted more than 24 marshalling yards over a 38,000-square-mile area through the very heart of the Reich.

A sensational new technique was used for the first time known by the heavy bombers Swooping down from their usual bombing level of about 25,000 feet, they smashed their targets from 1,500 feet.

Medium bombers from the 9th Air Force and the RAF 2nd Tactical Air Force also took part in the mass attacks, together with fighter-bombers from the U.S. 1st Tactical Air Force and RAF Fighter Command.

Marshalling Yards Pounded

Marshalling yards pounded by the 8th - in a wide area bounded on the west by Hanover, Hamburg and Kassel, and on the east by Berlin and Leipzig - were at Luneburg, Stendal, Halberstadt, Ludwislust, Uelzen, Salzwedel, Wittemberge, Hildesheim, Kneisen, Peine, Northeim, Vienenburg, Sangerhausen, Gottingen, and other vital points.

Lancasters and Halifaxes, as well as Liberators and Fortresses, for the first time broke into groups of three or four aircraft and flew at 1,500 to 2,000 feet to pinpoint railway bridges, small junctions and dispersed sidings.

The huge campaign extended all the way to the Danish peninsula, where night-flying Mosquitos hit the Danish-German border town of Flensburg.

Confusion reigned throughout Germany as, first, German "Achtung" broadcasts reported small groups of every type of Allied aircraft penetrating over Germany at the same time - from the south and all along the West Front - until they blanketed the western part of the country. Then frantic reports began trickling through the German communications network of hundreds of cuts in railway lines from Denmark to Italy.

Tenth Straight Day

Heavy bombers of the 15th Air Force flew on their tenth straight day to pound rail targets in Germany, Austria and Northern Italy, including railway lines radiating from Munich.

The paralyzing assaut[sic] was unrivalled in aerial history except for the opening of the Normandy invasion, when Allied planes carried out 13,000 sorties over a 25-hour period.

The 8th's objectives were scattered through the center of Germany in a rectangular area. Fortresses of Brig. Gen. Howard M. Turner's 1st Division pounded targets in the northern third; Liberators of Maj. Gen. William E. Kepner's 2nd

Division struck at the central third; and Fortresses
of Maj. Gen. E. Partridge's 3rd Division attached
targets in the southern third.

End of clipping

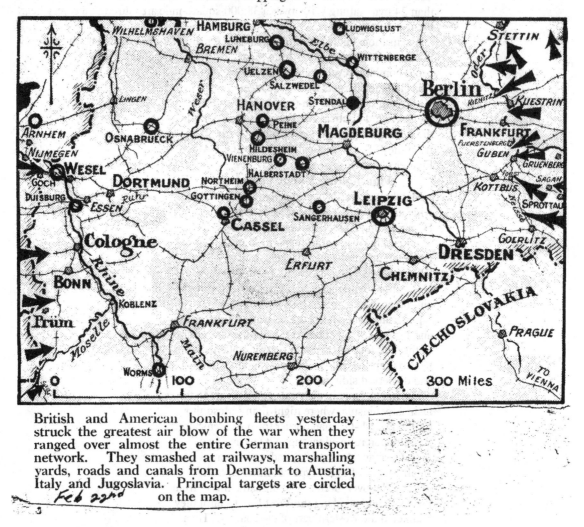

British and American bombing fleets yesterday
struck the greatest air blow of the war when they
ranged over almost the entire German transport
network. They smashed at railways, marshalling
yards, roads and canals from Denmark to Austria,
Italy and Jugoslavia. Principal targets are circled
Feb 22nd on the map.

[The map above is from Lt. Raber's scrapbook which had the same newspaper clipping as Lt. Harvey but
his included the map. Note that it indicates it is also from Feb 22. - grh]

===

FEBRUARY 23
BREAKFAST AT 300. BRIEFING AT 400. OFF TO MEININGEN, GERMANY.

TOTAL TIME 11 HRS [sic]. INSTRUMENT TAKE-OFF. NO FIGHTERS. FLAK SEEN TWICE - ONCE
NORTH OF STRAUSBERG AND AGAIN OVER STRAUSBERG. HIT SHIPS HYDRAULIC LINE.
ONE SHIP'S RADIO OPERATOR GOT LEG BLOWN OFF. SAW SWISS ALPS. CAME HOME THRU
[sic] FRANCE. LEFT FORMATIONS IN FRANCE AND CAME HOME AT LOW POWER DUE TO
FUEL SHORTAGE. FLEW HOME ON INSTRUMENTS. LANDED WITH ABOUT 200 GALS GAS. A

GOOD MISSION BUT NO NEED FOR GETTING FLAK. TODAY, AGAIN, WE BOMBED FROM 12,000 FEET.

TODAY I AM A HERO - I GOT MY AIR MEDAL.

MISSION #6 COMPLETE.

[As noted by S/Sgt Jorgenson, they are not flying the "Out House Mouse" on this mission and as noted in the April 25 Pilsen mission, the "Out House Mouse" did not have hydraulic flight controls. On the early B-17, hydraulics were used only for the engine cowling and brakes. Also, no additional information is available on the apparent verbal "flak" received at debriefing.

Mission planners carefully calculated the amount of fuel needed for each mission for an airplane carrying less fuel could carry more bombs and bombing WAS the objective. This fact, and the fact that this mission has the longest duration, means that it may have been this mission that is one of the few times I heard my father relate any of his flying experiences. While looking at his mission map in his scrapbook, I noticed one mission line that seemed to be about twice as long as all the others. He told me of a long mission where unknown to the crew, a strong tail wind had developed after they were airborne and it took them well beyond the intended target area. Since visibility was poor and all the ground features seemed to match their briefing information, they made their bomb runs and dropped their bombs. Of course on the return flight they were now flying into that wind. Because of the poor visibility from time to time he would drop down below the clouds to try and determine their location. After several of these attempts they finally broke through the clouds and saw the English Channel. While this was a welcome sight, all the fuel gauges were now reading empty. As they approached the white cliffs of Dover, he coaxed the last remaining burst of energy to gain the necessary altitude to clear the cliffs. Upon landing, they saw that the under-carriage of the aircraft was full of small leaves and twigs from their low clearance of the cliffs and the ground crew's fuel sticks all came up dry when they performed their routine check of the fuel tanks.

Marty Raber provided some confirmation of this when he informed me that on his mission map, the Hof mission has one of the longer mission lines. – grh]

From the diary of Lt. Phil Darby:

Mission #4
Today we bombed Meiningen. Were briefed for Hof, but the weather socked in. Caught light flak at Strasburg (on Rhine River). We got one hit; a hydraulic line in right wing. Bandits in the air, but we didn't see them. 10 hours in the air.

From the diary of Lt. Marty Raber:

Went to Hof. (At 12,000'. Supposed to bomb). Target overcast so bombe'd target of opportunity. We were to bomb RR again. Target hit was [remainder of line is blank — grh]. Little Flak encountered just before crossing lines below Strassburg. No Fighters.

From the diary of Lt. Paul Katz:

Up over Germany again today. This was mission number 5. It was the same as yesterday. Low altitude. We weren't as lucky today though and caught a little Flak. The lead ship made a mistake and went over a Flak area instead of around it. We got one hole in our wing. These low missions scare me. I sit and pray during the whole mission. If the enemy ever gets their guns on us at that height we are goners.

From the diary of S/Sgt Niel Jorgenson:

Fifth Mission

Place - Hof ... [I could not read the rest of the entry - grh]

Altitude - 25,000 feet
Flak - Little innacurate [sic]
Fighters - P-51 escourt [sic]

Troubles Encountered - None

Ships Name – 401st

[Name unknown, but the ship was from the 401st Squadron which is also at Bassingbourn - grh]

"Mission Sheet" of S/Sgt George Odenwaller

MISSION:	#4
TARGET:	SUPPORT OF PATTON's 3rd DIVISION (MEININGEN - HILDBURGHAUSEN)
FLAK:	MODERATE
FIGHTERS:	NONE
DAMAGE:	NONE
TAKE-OFF:	7:20
E.T.R:	5:30
OXYGEN TIME:	8 HOURS
T.T:	10 HOURS - 10 MIN
BOMB LOAD:	10 500LB G.P.'s & 2 400LB LEAFLET BOMBS
ALT:	13,000 FT
SHIP No:	557
NAME:	[None shown - grh]
TEMP:	- 20 F.

ANOTHER LOW ONE! SAW GERMAN FLAK GUNS SHOOTING UP AT US FROM LINES. LEAD SHIP FEATHERED ONE ENGIN [sic] - LANDED IN BELGIUM. VERY LONG MISSION. GAS VERY LOW ON WAY BACK - SAW THE SWISS ALPS FOR THE FIRST TIME: VERY BEAUTIFUL! DEAD TIRED!

From the diary of S/Sgt Walter Limberger:

#4
Target – Hildburg, Ger.
Flak – Moderate
Fighters – None
Damage – None
Take Off – 07:20
Landed – 1730 hrs
Total Time – 10 hrs 10 min
Oxygen – 8 hrs
Bombs – 10-500 lb. G.P.'s
Altitude – 13,000 ft.
Ship # – 557 No Name
Temp – -20°

Another low mission. Had flak over the front lines at Strasburg. Our lead ship feathered an engine and landed in belguim [sic]. We made it O.K. although our tanks were low on fuel. Longest mission so far. Was very tired on account of long time on oxygen.

NEWSPAPER CLIPPING (source unknown):

1,200 Heavies Continue Blitz on Reich Railways
* * *   * * *   * * *

Germa [remainder of line is unknown – grh]

—

Crews Say
Good Hits
Snarl Lines

The back-breaking blitz on German railway lines, slowed up somewhat Thursday night because of bad weather, roared anew yesterday afternoon when over 1,250 Fortresses and Liberators of the 8th Air Force dropped a pulverizing load of bombs on approximately 20 marshalling yards in southeastern Germany while heavy bombers of the RAF pummeled the communications center of Essen and hit a benzol plant at Geilenkirchen.

The 15th Air Force was out, too, heavies ranging from their bases in Italy to attach German communications for the 11th straight day, hitting rail lines at Vienna, Innsbruck, Klagenfurt and Villach.

The Fortresses and Liberators, again Carrying out their missions from medium altitudes of from 6,000 to 15,000 feet, blasted yards in five towns situated on rail lines radiating from the key transport center of Nuremburg, at which the 8th struck two mighty blows earlier in the week. The attack thus took the form of a mopping up operation, in which the bombers, having paralyzed the hub of this section of German communications, reached out to disable its smaller component parts.

The complete pattern of yesterday's assault by the 8th covered an area stretching from Schweinfurt south to Nuremburg and east to the Czech border, a much more compressed area than the one hit in Thursday's savage blow.

Crews returning from yesterday's raids, which took in the towns of Ansbach, Crailshelm, Kitzengen, Neumarkt, Schweinfurt and Treuchtlingen, reported rough weather on the way in, but fair visibility over the targets, with breaks in clouds over some yards affording good views for bombardiers. Some who saw the results of their bombing said they saw big red flashes burst in the yards, with rails, locomotives and cars knocked askew.

The protecting force of 650 Mustangs and Thunderbolts peeled off as usual to pour bullets and shells into airfields and rail yards along the route of attack. They destroyed 14 aircraft on the ground and caused severe damage to locomotives and other rolling

Rail lines at Luneburg, Germany, junction of a main route for reinforcement and supply of Nazi armies in the West, comprised one target of the massive raid Thursday. The air assault was one of the greatest in history, with more than 6,000 Allied war planes taking part.

stock. The bombers, which met no air opposition, and little flak, dropped a total of 3,250 tons on their objectives.

Damage reports on Thursday's great raids, which were carried out at from 6,000 to 15,000 feet and not at 1,500 feet as erroneously reported yesterday, revealed that great destruction was leveled on all targets hit, torn rails and blasted rolling stock, repair shops and roundhouses showing up in the photographs. Eight bombers and 19 fighters were missing from the raids.

End of Clipping

FEBRUARY 24
BREAKFAST AT 3:10 BRIEFING AT 4:10 OFF TO HAMBERG, GERMANY. BOMBED SUBMARINE PENS. FLAK MODERATE AND INACCURATE. SCREENING FORCE OF 12-B-17's WENT IN 5000 FT. LOW TO DROP CHAF. MISSION A SUCCESS. GROUPS PARTY IN EVENING. QUITE DULL

FOR A CHANGE. GOT A COMPLIMENT TODAY - "ONLY GOOD LANDING MADE IN THE SQUADRON WAS SHIP 841 - Lt. HARVEY."

7-1/2 HR. MISSION.

MISSION #7 COMPLETE

[George Odenwaller told me that Lt. Harvey was known for consistently "greasing the runway" - landing so smoothly, you would not hear the wheels hit the runway. "Ship 841" probably refers to the last 3-digits of the aircrafts tail number which agrees with S/Sgt Odenwaller's diary information. Per Plane Names & Fancy Noses, the only aircraft number ending in 841 known to have been assigned to the 91st is 338841 "Judy's Little Ass" which was assigned to the 323rd. - grh]

From the diary of Lt. Phil Darby:

Mission #5
Hamburg today. The target was overcast so their radar guns were fairly inaccurate. That chaf I am convinced is good stuff. Flak was quite a ways off. There are 144 guns there. Hope we never bomb it visually.

[Al Kus the waist gunner, told me that it was often his job to throw "piles" of chaff out his waist gun window as they neared the target area. Chaff was small pieces of aluminum foil he said reminded him of short pieces of aluminum foil commonly used to decorate a Christmas tree. Many times he had so many boxes of the stuff in the small waist he could barely move around to man his waist gun. The chaff caused interference with the radar guidance system used by the German flak gunners and per Marty Raber, at times was so effective the flak bursts were 5-miles away from the bomber stream. – grh]

From the diary of Lt. Marty Raber:

Bombed oil Refinery at Hamburgh by PFF. If visual was to bomb sub pens & factory. Flak was heavy but very inaccurate due to chaf. Was a good mission.

From the diary of Lt. Paul Katz:

Mission number six today. Today we raided Hamburg at 25,000 ft. It usually is a tough mission, but today the Flak was inaccurate. The whole mission took only 5 hours as compared with 10 hours yesterday. Today I got the Air Medal. It is awarded after six missions with [an oak-leaf] cluster for every six after that. Most people don't think much of it as it is an automatic award, but I prize it highly. I think anyone who lives through six missions deserves something. Tomorrow is our stand down day. We fly three times (if the weather is good). That means three days in a row (like the last three) and rest one. I am glad as I can use a rest after the last three raids.

From the diary of S/Sgt Niel Jorgenson:

Sixth Mission

Place - Hamburg

Flak - Fairly Heavy
Fighters - 4 grps [groups – grh] P-51's

Damage - None

Troubles Encountered - None

Ships Name - "Out House Mouse"

"Mission Sheet" of S/Sgt George Odenwaller:

MISSION: *#5*
TARGET: *HAMBURG*
FLAK: *MODERATE*
FIGHTERS: *NONE*
DAMAGE: *NONE*
TAKE-OFF: *8:45*
E.T.R: *3:45*
OXYGEN TIME: 4 HOURS
T.T: *7 HOURS*
BOMB LOAD: 12 500LB G.P.'s
ALT: *25,000 FT*
SHIP No: *841*
NAME: *[None shown]*
TEMP: *- 42 F.*

FIRST SHORT ONE! FLAK WAS BOXED AND INACCURATE. HAMBURG QUITE A LARGE PLACE. FLAK NOT VERY ACCURATE - MUCH "CHAFF" THROWN OUT. NO GROUP LOSSES. 300th GROUP MISSION TODAY!

From the diary of S/Sgt Walter Limberger:

#5
Target – Hamburg, Ger.
Flak – Moderate
Fighters – None
Damage – None
Take Off – 08:45
Landed – 1545 hrs

Total Time – 7 hrs
Oxygen – 4 hrs
Bombs – 12-500 lb General Purpose
Altitude – 25,000 ft.
Ship # – 841 No Name
Temp – -42°

Easy mission and it seemed good. Plenty of flak but wasn't very accurate as we threw out a lot of chaff. All our group landed back at base safely. We could take more of these.

NEWSPAPER CLIPPING - (Source unknown)

Rail-Hitting Heavies Tear Into Munich

The aerial sledgehammer fashioned by bombers of the 8th and 15th Air Forces and the RAF fell on German communications and fuel supplies for the fourth day in a row yesterday as 1,150 Fortresses and Liberators of the 8th hit railyards, airfields, an oil storage depot and a tank plant while Lancasters of the RAF bombed a synthetic oil plant near Dortmund and the 15th's heavies attacked communications at Linz, Austria.

The Big target for the 8th yesterday was Munich, a focal point in the German railway system, where Fortresses rumbled over in two waves to hit the terminal rail station and marshalling yards in the eastern and western parts of the city. Other formations of Fortresses pounded yards at Ulm while Liberators bombed the yards and a tank assembly plan[sic] at Aschaffenburg, and airfields at Giebelstadt and Schwebisch-Hall, west of Nurenburg. Fortresses also hammered an underground oil storage depot hidden in the woods outside Neuberg, between Munich and Nuremburg.

Fighters in Strafing Action

More than 700 Mustangs and Thunder-bolts of the 8th were out yesterday, 500 of them shielding the bombers, while a separate force of 200 Mustangs went on a strafing sweep over north central Germany, riddling locomotives and other rolling stock and shooting up airfields. The 55th Mustang Group caught eight jet-propelled Me262's taking off from a field near Giebelstadt, knocking down seven of them.

The fighters got 21 enemy craft in the air all told, eight of them jets, and destroyed another 20 on the ground. No Luftwaffe planes attacked the bombers, but the fighters, who ranged over wide areas, ran into several scattered formations of Nazi planes.

It was the fifth consecutive day that the 8th had dispatched more than 1,000 bombers. Over 1,100 Fortresses and Liberators, escorted by 500 Mustangs, were out Saturday, attacking oil refineries at Misburg, Hamburg and Harburg, rail targets in northwest Germany and submarine construction yards at Bremen and Hamburg. This followed a night in which RAF Bomber Command sent out more than 1,100 planes to batter communications, industrial and aviation targets.

End of Clipping

===

FEBRUARY 25
GROUP STAND-DOWN. SCHOOL IN P.M. AND EVENING WENT TO PICTURES.

From the diary of Lt. Phil Darby:

A group stand down today. Played some cribbage and wrote a few letters.

From the diary of Lt. Paul Katz:

No mission today. It is a group stand down which means we will get our squadron stand down tomorrow.

===

FEBRUARY 26
PRACTICE G.H. MISSION. RODE CO-PILOT FOR LT. ADAMS.
CAMBRIDGE IN EVENING.
SQUADRON STAND-DOWN TODAY.

59

From the diary of Lt. Phil Darby:

No flying today. I seem to have lost all desire to visit town. These missions have easily absorbed most of my energy.

From the diary of Lt. Marty Raber:

Stood down

From the diary of Lt. Paul Katz:

Squadron stand down today.

===

FEBRUARY 27
BREAKFAST AT 6:00 BRIEFING AT 7:00. OFF TO LIPZIG, GERMANY
NO FIGHTERS SEEN. FLAK LITE[sic] AND INACCURATE. BOMBED MARSHALLING YARDS IN
CENTER OF CITY. BOMB LOAD 10-500 LB GENERAL PURPOSE AND 2-M17 INCENDARY
BOMBS.
FLEW OWN SHIP TODAY.
9 HOUR MISSION

MISSION #8 COMPLETE.

From the diary of Lt. Phil Darby:

Mission #6
We hit Leipzig today - one of the strongly defended targets in Germany. We were after a war plant in No. West section of city, but the target was overcast so we bombed center of city by instrument. There was intense barrage flak just before we got over the city, but it strangely ceased as our group went over.

From the diary of Lt. Marty Raber:

Stood down

[This is the first diary entry where Lt. Raber is not with his crew. – grh]

From the diary of Lt. Paul Katz:

We are off again. Today it was Leipzig which is pretty close to the Russian lines. It is supposed to be heavily guarded by Flak guns. It was undercast[sic] though and what Flak they did throw up was inaccurate. Everyone got back safely. It was more or less a milk run

[A "milk run" is an easy mission – grh]

"Mission Sheet" of S/Sgt George Odenwaller:

MISSION: #6
TARGET: LEIPZIG
FLAK: MODERATE
FIGHTERS: NONE
DAMAGE: NONE
TAKE-OFF: 9:35
E.T.R: 6:45
T.T: 9 HOURS - 10 Min.
OXYGEN TIME: 6 HOURS
ALT: 26,500 FT
SHIP No: 636
NAME: OUTHOUSE MOUSE OR-N
TEMP: - 36 F.

    THOUGHT IT WAS GOING TO BE A ROUGH ONE - TURNED OUT TO BE THE WELL KNOWN "MILK RUN". FLAK HIGH ABOVE US & FAR BELOW. DAMNED GLAD IT WAS !

From the diary of S/Sgt Walter Limberger:

#6
Target – Leipzig, Ger.
Flak – Moderate
Fighters – None
Damage – None
Take Off – 09:35 hrs
Landed – 1845 hrs
Total Time – 9 hrs 10 min
Oxygen – 6 hrs
Bombs – 6-500 lb G. P.'s and 4 Clusters (M-17's)
Altitude – 26,500 ft.
Ship # – 636 Out House Mouse
Temp – -36°

Thought this was going to be rough, but it turned out to be long and fairly nice. The flak was quite heavy over the target, but inaccurate. Leipzig used to be a very rough target.

Article from the London Edition of <u>THE STARS AND STRIPES</u> Vol 5 No 100-1d
Wednesday Feb 28, 1945

1,100 Heavies
Keep Blitzing
Reich's Rails

Carrying their relentless attack on Germany into it ninth consecutive day, more than 1,100 heavy bombers of the 8th Air Force raided Nazi rail lines yesterday for the eighth time in their new offensive, 750 Fortresses pouring it on the traffic center at Leipzig while 350 Liberators attacked the marshalling yards at Halle, 20 miles northeast of Leipzig.

While the 8th hammered its targets, the 15th Air Force and the RAF made it a three-ply blow. Liberators and Fortresses of the 15th cut through intense flak to smash railway yards at Augsburg and a strong force of Halifaxes and Lancasters of the RAF attached the railway center of Mainz, on the left bank of the Rhine, near Frankfurt, and a benzol plant near Gelsenkirchen.

Fortresses of the 8th, again bombing through clouds, lined up on the largest main station in Europe in flying over Liepzig. Huge sidings, crowded with warehouses and locomotive repair shops, fan out from the station for more than 430 acres. From the station stem[sic] main lines going to Berlin, Breslau, Dresden, Munich, Frankfurt, the Rhur and the Rhineland.

Vast Marshalling Yards

Halle, on the main line from Berlin to Frankfurt, has vast marshalling yards and repair facilities. Libs which struck these yards through clouds included the veteran 93rd Bomb Group, which racked up its 350th mission yesterday. In its 29 months of activity, the 93rd participated in the invasions of North Africa, Sicily, Italy and Normandy and bombing of the Ploesti oil refineries.

The escort of more than 700 Thunderbolts and Mustangs continued strafing enemy airfields and rail lines yesterday, reporting destruction of more than 70 parked aircraft and damaging of 44 locomotives and 154 rail cars. One squadron of the 353rd Mustang Group, finding a hole in the clouds near Weimar, swooped down to make a spectacular raid over an airfield, leaving more than 50 planes burning, of which 36 were destroyed. Nobody on the field, on which all types of craft, even a battered Flying Fortress, were parked, made a move to resist.

In Monday's attack on Berlin, from which 16 bombers and seven fighters are missing, the 8th may have dropped its 500-pound "Goop" bomb, an incendiary that defies all extinguishing devices, The Associated Press reported yesterday, quoting officials in Washington. USSTAF said last night it had no knowledge of the bomb being in use Monday.

A Reuter dispatch from Stockholm reported huge fires started in the three railway terminals hit by the 8th, with many freight cars, loaded with food, munitions and other supplies for the Russian front, destroyed.

End of Clipping

==

FEBRUARY 28
PAY DAY AND ALL DEBTS PAID OFF - JUST ABOUT. STOOD-DOWN TODAY. WENT TO MICKY TRAINER (RADAR BOMBING) IN P.M. FLEW SLO-TIME JOB FOR 3 HRS.

["slo-time" means non-combat flying usually associated with some training or logistical activity. As Lt. Darby notes in his diary, this case was to ferry another ship back to Bassingbourn. – grh]

From the diary of Lt. Phil Darby:

The crew (with the exception of Raber bombardier) didn't fly. I went to a replacement depot with Hoffman. We flew a ship back to the field.

[Lt. Darby notes that Lt. Raber is now an exception. – grh]

From the diary of Lt. Marty Raber:

Bombed "Schwerte".
Target RR Yards inconjunction with crippling transportation. Saw Flak but we had none. It was a milk run. Bombing was done th[r]ough clouds by instruments.

[This is the first of Lt. Raber's diary entries where he is obviously not flying with his assigned crew. – grh]

From the diary of Lt. Paul Katz:

I am not flying today. The squadron is overstaffed and we may not have to fly on every mission form[sic] now on.

==

MARCH 1
BREAKFAST AT 630, BRIEFING AT 730. OFF TO HEILBRONN, GERMANY.
FLAK LITE[sic] AND ACCURATE BUT HIT ONLY THE HIGH SQD. FLEW THRU A WARM FRONT ON RETURN. QUITE A SUCCESSFUL MISSION. LANDED AT 1900 HRS. UPON RETURN. 9-1/2 HR MISSION.

PICTURES IN EVENING. "MY REPUTATION".

MISSION #9 COMPLETE.

From the diary of Lt. Phil Darby:

Mission #7
Heilbronn was todays mission. We hit the marshalling yard with limited downward visibility. Got some flak when we crossed the zones, very near Rhine now.

From the diary of Lt. Marty Raber:

Went to bomb RR yards at Heilbonn[sic]. Encountered no Flak over target. Had light inaccurate Flak over lines. (Milk Run).

From the diary of Lt. Paul Katz:

Off to raid Heilbronn today. Not much excitement. We got a little Flak hit it did not hit our squadron. The mission went off very well. It was number 8 for me.

"Mission Sheet" of S/Sgt George Odenwaller:

MISSION:	*#7*
TARGET:	*HEILBRONN*
FLAK:	*LITTLE: OVER LINES*
FIGHTERS:	*NONE*
DAMAGE:	*NONE*
TAKE-OFF:	*9:45*
E.T.R:	*7:00*
T.T:	*9 HOURS - 15 Min.*
OXYGEN TIME: 4 HOURS	

BOMB LOAD: 8 500 LB. G.P.'s & 4 CLUSTERS
ALT: 20,000 FT
SHIP No: 636
NAME: OUTHOUSE MOUSE OR-N
TEMP: - 24 F..

SAW GUNFIRE BELOW, (OUR LINES) BUT DIDN'T REALIZE THE KRAUTS WERE THROWING FLAK UP AT US ! VERY LIGHT & INACCURATE. SAW THE ALPS AGAIN - BEAUTIFUL !

From the diary of S/Sgt Walter Limberger:

#7

Target – Heilbronn, Ger.

Flak – Over front lines

Fighters – None

Damage – None

Take Off – 09:45

Landed – 1900

Total Time – 9 hrs 15 min

Oxygen – 4 hrs

Bombs – 8-500 lb G. P.'s and 4-M17 Clusters

Altitude – 20,000 ft.

Ship # – 636 Out House Mouse

Temp – -24°

What an easy mission this one was. A milk run as they're called. No flak over target, ut some over front lines. Flew near the Swiss Alps again. What a beautiful sight.

NEWSPAPER CLIPPING - (Source unknown)

Blitz Goes On,
Rails Pounded

Allied air fleets continued their cease-
less blitz on Germany's communications lines
yesterday when the 8th Air Force, getting away
more than 1,000 bombers for the eighth
consecutive day, sent out over 1,200 Fortresses
and Liberators in an attack on eight rail centers
in southern Germany while Lancasters and
Halifaxes of the RAF hit the transportation

center of Mannheim and a synthetic oil plant at
Kamen, near Dortmund.

Meanwhile, the 15th Air Force, having
dropped a record tonnage of bombs on Brenner
Pass rail lines in the previous 24 hours, roared
into Austria again as Liberators and Fortresses
attacked the well-battered Moosbierbaum oil
refinery, 22 miles northwest of Vienna. The
Luftwaffe, rising to thwart the 15th's growing
attempt to seal Kesselring's troops in Italy,
clashed with a strong escort of fighters which
destroyed five Nazi planes.

Targets for the 8th's bombers, which had an
escort of 450 Mustangs, were Heilbronn,
Bruchsal, Coppingen, Reutlingen, Neckarsulm,
Igolstadt, Ulm, and Augsburg, all located near
Stuttgart and Munich. Some of the heavies had
to contend with heavy cloud, bombing through
instruments.

The 8th had 1,100 heavies out Saturday,
hitting four oil refineries, two synthetic oil
plants and industrial and rail targets in a wide
area of Germany, including the bomb-marked
rail yards at Chemnitz and an oil plant 27 miles
north of Dresden, described by German
Overseas News Agency yesterday as a mass of
ruins after concentrated attacks by the 8th and
the RAF. Some fighters opposed the bombers,
but failed to break through the shield of 700
Mustangs and Thunderbolts.

Three bombers and two fighters are missing
from yesterday's raid, and 19 bombers and six
fighters from Saturday. Friday's losses,
previously unreported, were 14 bombers and 10
fighters.

End of Clipping

===

MARCH 2
SQUADRON STAND-DOWN. FLEW THE RUNWAY LOCALIZER IN P.M. GROUND SCHOOL IN
A.M.

[Suspect the "runway localizer" is an early form of radar approach. The "localizer" in a modern I.L.S
(Instrument Landing System) provides the directional bearing for the pilot to line up with the runway. This,
combined with a separate vertical signal, provides the pilot with the electronic "Glide Path". I believe his
April 24 entry where he states the "glide path was out" confirms this conclusion. – grh]

From the diary of Lt. Phil Darby:

A squadron stand down today so I've rested and written letters.

From the diary of Lt. Paul Katz:

Stood down both days. Flew some practice missions.

[Another multi-dated entry dated March 2, 3, 1945 – grh]

==

MARCH 3
STOOD-DOWN TO DAY[sic] SINCE WE WERE A SPARE CREW.
SLEPT MOST OF THE DAY.
WENT TO TOWN IN EVENING.

[A "spare crew" was one who was fully prepared and briefed to fly a mission if for any reason one of the scheduled crews was not available. A spare crew was one who would otherwise be standing-down. – grh]

From the diary of Lt. Phil Darby:

The crew didn't fly on today's mission to Dresden. Joe and I test hopped a plane with four new engines. We also practiced flying the runway localizer.

From the diary of Lt. Marty Raber:

We hit Ruhland supposedly but weather prevented it. We were to bomb an oil refinery. We really bombed a RR Yard at Chemnitz. It was by instrument. What Flak encountered was light & inaccurate.

[Lt. Raber's second diary entry where he is flying with another crew. – grh]
==

MARCH 4
BREAKFAST AT 315, BRIEFING AT 415. OFF TO ULM, GERMANY.
ULM IS OR WAS ONE OF THE OLDEST TOWNS IN GERMANY.
BOMBED TANK AND ARMORED VEHICLE FACTORY. NO FLAK AND NO FIGHTERS.
9 HR. MISSION.

MISSION #10 COMPLETE.

From the diary of Lt. Phil Darby:

Mission #8
Waded thru [sic] heavy con-trails and a lot of scattered clouds to bomb Ulm on instruments. Didn't see a burst of flak all day. Ulm has vital rail linkages and is near Lake Constance in extreme southern end of Germany. We were five miles from Swiss border at one time.

From the diary of Lt. Marty Raber:

Supposed to bomb a oil refinery at Ulm. It was overcast so we hit the secondary which was a R.R. yard at Ulm. There was no Flak at all. We assembled over France.

From the diary of Lt. Paul Katz:

Today we hit Ulm. It is one of the oldest towns in Germany. We went after a tank and armored vehicle factory. No Flak or Fighters [sic]. *Number 9 is over.*

From the diary of S/Sgt Niel Jorgenson:

Seventh Mission

Target - Ulm, Germany

Flak - None
Fighters - None. Four grps [groups - grh] P-51's, 47's per Division

Damage - None

Troubles Encountered - #3 engine ran rough, changed #2 engine's electronic turbo amplifier

Ships Name - "Out House Mouse"

"Mission Sheet" of S/Sgt George Odenwaller:

MISSION:	*#8*
TARGET:	*ULM*
FLAK:	*NONE*
FIGHTERS:	*NONE*
DAMAGE:	*NONE*
TAKE-OFF:	*6:45*
E.T.R:	*5:30*
T.T:	*9 HOURS*
OXYGEN TIME:	*5 HOURS - 5 MIN.*
BOMB LOAD:	*8 500 LB. G.P.'s & 4 M-17 CLUSTERS & LEAFLETS*
ALT:	*26,000 FT*
SHIP No:	*636*
NAME:	*OUTHOUSE MOUSE OR-N*
TEMP:	*- 24 F..*

ANOTHER "MILK RUN" - NO FLAK OVER THE TARGET. RAN INTO ABOUT 50 PUFFS OF SPREAD OUT FLAK WHILE LETTING DOWN OVER THE LINES. SAW THE ALPS AGAIN - REALLY

SOMETHING TO SEE. GOOD FIGHTER SUPPORT. THE I.P. WAS LAKE CONSTANCE, SWITZERLAND. VERY COLD TODAY !!

From the diary of S/Sgt Walter Limberger:

#8
Target – Ulm, Germany
Flak – None
Fighters – None
Damage – None
Take Off – 0645
Landed – 15:50
Total Time – 9 hrs 5 min
Oxygen – 5 hrs
Bombs – 8-500 lb G. P.'s and 4-M-17 Incendiary's
Altitude – 26,000 ft.
Ship # – 636 Out House Mouse
Temp – -40°

Another easy mission. Not one flak burst from my position anyway. No fighters. Flew over scenic Swiss Alps again. The I.P. (Initial Point) was Lake Constance. Only thing, it was too cold at altitude today -40°

NEWSPAPER CLIPPING - (Source unknown)

1,000 Heavies Keep Blitzing Rails and Oil

Bombing through cloud so thick that most crewmen said the "didn't see an inch of German ground," more than 1,000 Fortresses and Liberators of the 8th Air Force, many of them forced back by the weather before reaching their targets, carried the 8th Air Force's blitz on Nazi rails and industry into its 14th straight day yesterday with a blow aimed at objectives in Ulm and other points in southwest Germany.

No enemy planes were sighted and flak was so light that many bombers got through without encountering a single burst. But the weather easily made up for lack of opposition. Snow-covered targets, plus a dense ground haze, thick contrails and heavy cloud made bombing by instrument necessary.

Dove-tailed with 15th, RAF

Operations of the 8th, which sent 500 fighters along with the bombers, dove-tailed with the non-stop blows being struck by the RAF and the 15th Air Force. While Lancasters of the RAF assaulted marshalling yards at Wanne-Eickel in the Ruhr, Fortresses and Liberators of the 15th flew out on their 19th mission in the last 20 days, attacking rail lines in Austria and Hungary.

End of Clipping

===

MARCH 5

GROUP STAND-DOWN. S-2 [intelligence – grh] TOLD US TODAY THAT ON OUR MISSION TO HAMBERG, WE SUNK 5 NEW SUBMARINES AS WELL AS "WORKED" OVER THE PENS QUITE WELL.

FLEW LT. ADAM'S SHIP ("RAMBLIN REBEL") ON A TEST FLIGHT.

PICTURES IN EVENING AND A LETTER HOME.

[The Hamburg mission was flown Feb 24 – grh]

From the diary of Lt. Phil Darby:

Stood down today, but we flew slo-time for most of the afternoon. Chased clouds and flew formation with a P-51 and some stirlings.

From the diary of Lt. Paul Katz:

Group stand down today. Got a report on the Hamberg mission. We sunk[sic] 5 new subs as well as hitting the sub-pens.

===

MARCH 6
STAND-DOWN AGAIN. FLEW GROUPE[sic] FORMATION FOR A GENERAL TODAY. 48 HR. PASS
BEGINS TODAY AT 1700 HOURS.

From the diary of Lt. Phil Darby:

Practice formation today. About 3-hour mission.

From the diary of Lt. Paul Katz:

48 hour pass. Did not go any place. Just hung around camp.

[Entry dated March 6, 7, 8, 1945 – grh]
===

MARCH 7
ON PASS IN CAMBRIDGE. NO EXCITEMENT.

From the diary of Lt. Phil Darby:

*Last night I wandered the streets of London for four hours in search of a place to sleep. I met an
old man (75 yrs) in a pub near Temple Square. We chatted and drank beer until closing time. A
woman everyone called "Mom" (she had only five teeth) was especially helpful. At last I found a
cabby who drove me to the Saint _____ [his blank –grh] Hotel. Came very close to being a "flop
house". Red sheets on the bed and a horrid little man that bludgeoned the door to get me up at
0730 the next morning.*

*I met a flier in the meager lobby the following A.M. He and I went down town together. I secured
a room at the Jules Club Red Cross with Lt. Burkakoff. He had reservations with a Captain friend
but decided in my favor.*

*I saw Bob Amesbury at the Grosvenor House. Had a swell meal. I was lucky to get tickets for
"Strike It Again" with Sid Field. He's a marvelous comedian. Also saw "Practically Yours" (F.
MacMurry - C. Colbert). A ticket in the Royal Circle cost 11/6 - that's outrageous.*

*This evening, I found an American bar and got well plastered on Prin #2 (gin base) and everything
from burgundy to sherry and port. I spent the earlier part of the evening with a Warrant Officer,
RAF Glider Pilot, and Canadian Captain. The glider pilot and I went to the "Red Lion" pub to
finish the nite[sic]. Some Aussies were interesting to watch because they thought they had located a
sucker after I bought them a couple of drinks. A GI Private acted by self appointment as my
personal guardian.*

Met Ruth later. Maybe someday I'll spend two days in a row where women don't interfere.

==

MARCH 8
ON PASS STILL

From the diary of Lt. Phil Darby:

Climbed out of a warm bed at noon, cleaned up and went shopping. I didn't find a thing that interested me. Saw the picture "Keys of the Kingdom" with Gregory Peck. Dinner at the Grosvenor House where I met Major Inlow. He was my instructor at Kemper (Math, I believe). I'll have to catch an early train. Arrived at Kings Cross about five-thirty. Spent half-hour in a book store before I caught the "Royston Limited".

==

MARCH 9
DID NOT FLY. LISTED AS A SPARE.

HAD TRAINER IN P.M.

WENT TO PICTURES IN EVENING. "CAROLINA BLUES".

TODAY MAKES ONE MORE YEAR IN THE ARMY.

From the diary of Lt. Phil Darby:

A mission went to Kassel today. We were a spare and didn't fly.

From the diary of Lt. Marty Raber:

We hit RR yards at Cassel. It was a visual run. We plastered the target. The Flak was light but accurate.

[Lt. Raber's third diary entry where he is flying with another crew. – grh]

From the diary of Lt. Paul Katz:

No mission today. Went to ground school & trainer.

==

MARCH 10
BREAKFAST AT 545, BRIEFING AT 645. OFF TO SINSEN, GERMANY.
SHORT MISSION. NO FIGHTERS. FLAK LITE[sic] BUT DAMNED ACCURATE.
7 HR. MISSION.

MISSION #11 COMPLETE

From the diary of Lt. Phil Darby:

Mission #9
Today we bombed Sinsen at 25,000 ft. The target was obscured by clouds, but the flak was quite heavy and mostly inaccurate. Sinsen is in the Ruhr and close to Essen and Dortmund.

From the diary of Lt. Marty Raber:

We were to bomb RR junction at Sensin. 324th & 401st Did. We bombed Recklinghousen. It was an instrument job. Flak was light but accurate.

[Mission dates match, but actual targets do not. Lt. Raber is apparently with another crew. – grh]

From the diary of Lt. Paul Katz:

Up today to hit a rail yard at a small town just over the lines. The town was Sinsen. A short mission. I didn't see any Flak, but Joe tells me there was some pretty accurate bursts under us. No casualties: Number 10 is over.

From the diary of S/Sgt Niel Jorgenson:

Eighth Mission

Target - Sinsen, Germany

Flak - Inaccurate & far
Fighters - None Mosquitos & P-51 escourt [sic]

Damage - None

Troubles Encountered - None

Ships Name - "Out House Mouse"

"Mission Sheet" of S/Sgt George Odenwaller:

MISSION: *#9*

```
TARGET:        SIN SEN (TRYING TO BOMB IN FRONT OF PATTON !)
FLAK:          NONE
FIGHTERS:      NONE
DAMAGE:        NONE
TAKE-OFF:      9:30
E.T.R:         3:30
T.T:           6 HOURS
OXYGEN TIME: 4 HOURS
BOMB LOAD:   34 100 LB. G.P.'s & 2 M-17 CLUSTERS & LEAFLETS
ALT:           26,500 FT
SHIP No:       636
NAME:          OUTHOUSE MOUSE  OR-N
TEMP:          - 42 F.
```

NO FLAK AT ALL & NO FIGHTERS - NONE REPORTED IN THE AREA. SAW THE ALPS AGAIN - OUR I.P. WAS LAKE CONSTANCE IN SWITZERLAND: WAS COLD AS HELL UP THERE - MASK FROZE UP IN TURRET. ON OXYGEN CHECK, THE WAIST DID NOT REPLY - CAME UP OUT OF BALL & SAVED WAIST GUNNER'S LIFE: HIS MASK FROZE UP & WAS ALMOST GONE - TRIED TO FIGHT ME OFF AS I INCREASED HIS OXYGEN FLOW & SUPPLY.

NOTE:
    THIS REPLACEMENT WAIST GUNNER CAME OUT TO OUR A/C WEARING A FANCY BLACK LEATHER JACKET, SUN GLASSES (WHICH NEVER CAME OFF), BLACK LEATHER BOOTS & A "100 MISSION CRUSH" HAT ALONG WITH HIS EQUIPMENT BAG: A REAL "HOT SHOT". THIS GUY REPLACED AL KUS, OUR REGULAR WAIST GUNNER, FOR ONE MISSION ONLY. (A POOL GUNNER; NO CREW).

From the diary of S/Sgt Walter Limberger:

#9

Target – Sinsan, Ger.

Flak – Moderate

Fighters – None

Damage – None

Take Off – 09:30 hrs

Landed – 1530 hrs

Total Time – 6 hrs

Oxygen – 4 hrs

Bombs – 34-100 lb anti-personnel bombs and 2-M17 Clusters

Altitude – 26,000 ft.

Ship # – 636 Out House Mouse

Temp – -42°

Flak was fairly accurate, but there wasn't a great deal of it. A very short mission. We bombed in front of Patton's troops in close support. On some missions we have to abort as Patton's troops had taken out intended target.

Heavies Hit U-Boat Yards, Continue Blitz on Oil, Rails

Bombing through clouds, more than 1,200 Fortresses and Liberators of the 8th Air Force attacked German submarine construction yards at Bremen, Hamburg and Kiel yesterday and spiralled down loads on eight oil refineries in the two cities.

At the same time RAF heavies rose in strength to smite the railway and communications center of Essen, close to the Western Front, as 1,000 planes of RAF Bomber Command, carrying an escort of 200 fighters, blanketed the city with high explosives.

The raids climaxed a big weekend for both the 8th and the RAF. On Saturday more than 1,350 Forts and Libs continued the drive to cut Nazi communications to the Ruhr by aiming an assault at interlocking rail lines running from the area. Three marshalling yards in and near Dortmund and other targets north and east of the Ruhr were bombed, also through clouds.

In all, almost 4,000 planes of the 8th took part in the weekend activities, for 500 fighters escorted Saturday's raiders and 750 P47s and P51s formed yesterday's protective cloak. One bomber and two fighters failed to return Saturday and one bomber and three fighters were yesterday's losses.

U.S. heavies met no enemy air opposition, but intense flak was reported over all targets yesterday after a relatively light barrage Saturday.

Lancasters of the RAF were out in daylight Saturday, too, making a concentrated attack on the synthetic oil plant at Schelven-Buer. And Mosquitoes Saturday night hit Berlin for the 19th day in a row.

End of Clipping

MARCH 11
GROUP STAND-DOWN.

PICTURES IN EVENING, "MINISTER OF FEAR".

WORKED ON MODEL B-26.

WENT TO SEE AND "INSPECT" A BRITISH LANCASTER. QUITE AN AIRPLANE.

From the diary of Lt. Phil Darby:

Group stand down - I climbed out of the sack at noon. We went thru[sic] a Lancaster. It doesn't have any co-pilot and seems to be a fine airplane. The most noticeable thing to us is the lack of armor plate.

From the diary of Lt. Paul Katz:

Group standown [sic] today. No flying. Working on model airplane.

[S/Sgt Odenwaller once told me of a "ground-pounding" general who was being given a tour of Bassingbourn by his pilot son. While most of the "Out House Mouse" crew were in Lt. Katz's area of his barracks inspecting the workmanship on his latest model, the tour party entered and the son ask Lt. Harvey to introduce his father to the others in the group. Knowing how the "regular army" looked at officers fraternizing with enlisted men and without even the slightest hesitation, Lt. Harvey began – " **Lt.** Odenwaller, **Lt.** Kus, Lt. Katz, etc. until everyone had been introduced. The General briskly shook everyone's hand and was none the wiser since no one was in proper uniform. Lt. Harvey had "come around". – grh]

==

MARCH 12
BREAKFAST AT 540, BRIEFING AT 640. OFF TO DILLENBERG, GERMANY.
NO FLAK NOR FIGHTERS.
MY SONG FOR TO DAY[sic] HAS BEEN, "DOWN IN THE VALLEY". BROKE IN A NEW
BOMBARDIER (F/O GREEN) [a Field Officer named Green – grh] ON HIS FIRST MISSION. HE
SEEMED QUITE UNHAPPY ABOUT IT ALL.
MISSION A MILK RUN.
7-1/2 HR. MISSION.

MISSION #12 COMPLETE.

From the diary of Lt. Phil Darby:

Mission #10
What a divine mission it was. We bombed Dillingburg by GH methods. Quite uneventful for the most part.

From the diary of Lt. Paul Katz:

Mission 11 today. We hit the town of Dillenberg in the Rhur. There was no Flak today. It was a short mission, the kind I like. We hit the target through the clouds.

From the diary of S/Sgt Niel Jorgenson:

Eighth Mission

Target - Dillenberg, Germany

Flak - None
Fighters - None 4 grps of P-51 escourt

Damage - None

Troubles Encountered - None

      "MILK RUN"

Ships Name - "Out House Mouse"

"Mission Sheet" of S/Sgt George Odenwaller:

MISSION:	*#10*
TARGET:	*DILLENBERG*
FLAK:	*NONE*
FIGHTERS:	*NONE*
DAMAGE:	*NONE*
TAKE-OFF:	*09:30*
E.T.R:	*16:30*
T.T:	*7 HOURS*
OXYGEN TIME:	*4 HOURS.*
BOMB LOAD:	*34 100's & 2 M-17 CLUSTERS & LEAFLETS*
ALT:	*21,000 FT*
SHIP No:	*636*
NAME:	*OUTHOUSE MOUSE OR-N*
TEMP:	*- 29 F.*

From the diary of S/Sgt Walter Limberger:

#10
Target — Dillenburg, Ger.
Flak — None

Fighters – None
Damage – None
Take Off – 09:30 hrs
Landed – 1630 hrs
Total Time – 7 hrs
Oxygen – 4 hrs
Bombs – 34-100 lb anti-personnel and 2-M17 Incendiary Cluster
Altitude – 21,000 ft.
Ship # – 636 Out House Mouse

Another nice mission (milk run) as I didn't see a burst of flak from tail position. From a combat airmans point of view, these are O.K. We can't be this lucky forever!

From the back of the following clipping I obtained the following: Vol. 5, no. 111, March 13, 1945. Comparing this info to other clippings, the article appears to be from the London Edition of THE STARS AND STRIPES - grh.

Blitz Both Fronts
Heavies Hit
Near Rhine,
Along Baltic

Blaze of Glory

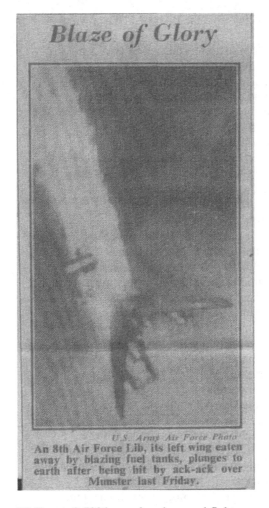

U.S. Army Air Force Photo

An 8th Air Force Lib, its left wing eaten away by blazing fuel tanks, plunges to earth after being hit by ack-ack over Munster last Friday.

Well over 3,500 heavy bombers and fighters of the 8th and 15th Air Forces and the RAF roared over Germany yesterday in attacks that shook the Reich from the Rhine to the Oder and south to Vienna.

The tremendous blow, spearheaded by the 8th in an assault that spread-eagled both Eastern and Western fronts, gave direct aid to U.S. and Russian troops battling on both approaches to the heart of Germany.

Half the force of 1,350 Fortresses and Liberators and 750 escorting fighters split to attack naval and military installations at the Baltic port of Swinemunde, 35 miles north of Stettin, and marshalling yards at six towns in an area about 60 miles east of the river opposite Cologne and Coblenz.

RAF Smashes Dortmund

While the 8th was blasting its string of targets in the Rhineland, more than 1,000 Halifaxes and Lancasters of the RAF, protected by a screen of Spitfires and Mustangs, struck 40 miles to the north, bombing the communications center of Dortmund, 15 miles east of Essen, which was

79

still smoking from the RAF's raid the previous day.

The 15th's effort, fashioned by Forts and Libs and a strong shield of fighters, was directed at oil installations in the Vienna area.

The attack on Swinemunde was the closest blow to the Eastern Front the 8th has yet delivered. It fell only 16 miles from where Marshal Zhukov's forces are striking for the Baltic port of Stettin. Plans for the attack were laid after photo reconnaissance three days ago showed the one-time seaside resort on the Oder estuary teeming with activity.

Clouds Obstruct View

Specific targets attacked were not disclosed and results were not observed because of heavy cloud. But the port is known to be a strong navel base, with shipyards and oil storage depots, and a likely base for the pocket battleship Adm. Scheer and U-boats which may have left the East Baltic.

The marshalling yards opposite the Rhine were at Siegen, Betzdorf, Dillenburg, Wetzlar, Friedburg, and Marburg. Here, too, as over Swinemunde, there was heavy cloud. Bombardiers used instruments over the targets.

One bomber and three fighters failed to return.

Last night, German radio broke out with ringing Achtungs, describing a strong force of fast enemy bombers approaching the Hanover-Brunswick area - "bomb alley" to Berlin - indicating that Mosquitoes were out to hit the capitol for the 21st successive night.

End of Clipping

===

MARCH 13
DIVISION STAND-DOWN TO DAY[sic]. VERY PEACEFUL DAY.
FLEW A SCS-51 (RUN WAY LOCALIZER) MISSION.
GAVE CO-PILOT DUAL INSTRUCTION.
WORKED ON B-26 IN EVENING.

From the diary of Lt. Phil Darby:

Division stand down, but I flew with Yavis in the morning (practice "Mickey" runs) and in Ushers D-Dog this afternoon (runway localizer).

["Ushers D-Dog" refers to aircraft OR-D. Per <u>The Ragged Irregulars of Bassingbourn</u>, Pg 223, at this time of the war this identified aircraft 338806 which had no name. This aircraft failed to return and landed on the continent March 22, 1945 and was salvaged March 25. - grh]

From the diary of Lt. Paul Katz:

Division squadron standown [sic] today, no flying.

===

MARCH 14
SQUADRON STAND-DOWN.
FLEW PRACTICE BOMBING MISSION (BLUE BOMB).

GOT A PAIR OF PINKS GREASY BY FLYING IN THEM - NEVER AGAIN!
SAW U.S.O. SHOW IN P.M. VERY POOR.
PICTURES IN EVENING.

["Pinks" are the light brown trousers of the Army's Class-A dress uniform – grh]

From the diary of Lt. Phil Darby:

We dropped blue bombs in the afternoon and had very little free time.

From the diary of Lt. Paul Katz:

Squadron standown [sic] , no flying.

===

MARCH 15
DID NOT FLY MISSION TODAY. SPARE CREW IN LEAD SQD. AND NO ONE FAILED TO SHOW UP.

WENT TO LINK TRAINER IN A.M.
WORKED ON B-26 IN P.M.
PICTURES IN EVENING.

From the diary of Lt. Phil Darby:

Marty and I went into Royston. My ear is bothering me again.

From the diary of Lt. Marty Raber:

We went to Oranienburg. We were to bomb RR yards. The whole 8th was split between two targets. We saw a lot of Flak but none hit us. The Flak over the target was heavy & accurate but they must have been reloading as we went over. Bombing was visual. The target hit. I saw one 17 go down & 7 chutes come out.

[The mission record of the 91st Bomb Group does report mission #314 to the Oranienburg marshalling yards on March 15. Lt. Darby may not have been correct on the date, or perhaps Lt. Raber and Lt. Darby went to Royston after Lt. Raber had completed his mission.

Perhaps George Odenwaller has explained this attitude best when he wrote to me saying: "Most people don't understand the combat thing with Air Corp combat crews – we were in the combat zone in England, but we had to fly many miles from that combat zone to engage the enemy. If we were lucky, we survived today only to shave and shower, get a date, and go to town as if no war existed! Tomorrow we did it all over again: Combat – Death so close each day – to survive and then sleep. Sleep was sometimes very difficult. We saw our friends from the other crews go down only a few hours ago. Will it be our turn tomorrow? And the booze really didn't do anything for you but block out tomorrow for a few hours. " - grh]

From the diary of Lt. Paul Katz:

Didn't fly today. The squadron did, but we were kept down for som[e] reason or other.

[Because Lt. Katz himself is confused, some readers may also be confused. Because they were the spare crew in the lead squadron, and because all men scheduled to fly showed up, Lt. Harvey's crew did not fly a mission today. – grh]

==

MARCH 16
BREAKFAST AT 515, BRIEFING AT 615. OFF TO LIPZIG, GERMANY.
MISSION SCRUBBED DUE TO WEATHER. HAD A LOAD OF NICKLES (PROPOGANDA LEAFLETTS) FOR BOMB LOAD.

SCRUBB #10

WORKED ON B-26 IN P.M. AND EVENING.

[A copy of a "Nickle" is available at the end of the diaries in the Scrap Book section. – grh]

From the diary of Lt. Phil Darby:

Mission to Berlin was scrubbed because of weather. My ear is bothering me a lot more now.

From the diary of Lt. Paul Katz:

Mission to Leipzig today but it was scrubbed before were got off the ground. Went to services this evening. This is the second time.

MARCH 17
BREAKFAST AT 420, BRIEFING AT 520. OFF TO BOHLIN, GERMANY. (11 MILES SOUTH OF
LIPZIG).
ATTACK AN SYNTHETIC OIL PLANT. TOWN OF 58,000 PEOPLE NEAR BY IN CASE WE MISS.
HEAVY WALL OF FLAK ON COURSE IN FRONT OF TARGET. SKY WAS BLACK WITH FLAK.
WE WERE NOT HIT SINCE WE WENT IN AT 30,000 FT. 10/10 OVERCAST. WENT THRU[sic] TWO
COLD FRONTS. FLEW MOST OF THE WAY IN FORMATION ON INSTRUMENTS. LANDED WITH
200 GAL OF GAS. LENGTH OF MISSION WAS 10 HRS.

MISSION #12A COMPLETE.

PICTURES IN EVENING. "BOWERY TO BROADWAY".

[Lt. Harvey numbers this mission as "12A" to avoid the unlucky number 13. – grh]

From the diary of Lt. Phil Darby:

Reported on Sick Call and was sent to hosp.[sic] *near Huntington.*

From the diary of Lt. Marty Raber:

Bohlen to bomb synthetic oil plant.
Flak Moderate and inaccurate. Was an instrument run.

From the diary of Lt. Paul Katz:

*Up for a mission. We went to Leipzig today. This was mission number 12 and gave me a
[oak-leaf] cluster for my air medal. It was a 10 hour mission which is a long time to be flying.
We didn't get any Flak until we got to the target. At the target they really thru*[sic] *it up.
It was the thickest I've seen but it wasn't accurate. We got back without any holes in the ship.*

"Mission Sheet" of S/Sgt George Odenwaller:

MISSION: *#11*
TARGET: *BOHLEN*
FLAK: *HEAVY, INTENSE, ACCURATE*
FIGHTERS: *NONE*

```
DAMAGE:          SOME
TAKE-OFF:        07:30
E.T.R:           17:00
T.T:             9 HRS - 30 MIN
OXYGEN TIME: 5 HOURS
BOMB LOAD:   8 500 LB. G.P.'s & 4 M-17 CLUSTERS
ALT:             31,500 FT
SHIP No:         636
NAME:            OUTHOUSE MOUSE  OR-N
TEMP:            - 65 F.
```

From the diary of S/Sgt Walter Limberger:

#11

Target — Bohlen, Ger.

Flak — Heavy - Intense - Accurate

Fighters — None

Damage — Some

Take Off — 07:30

Landed — 1700

Total Time — 9 hrs 30 min

Oxygen — 5 hrs

Bombs — 8-500 lb G. P.'s and 4-M17 Incendiary Clusters

Altitude — 31,500 ft.

Ship # — 636 Out House Mouse

Temp — -65°

It had to end. This one was rough as the flak gunners threw up enough flak to literally [sic] *walk on it. The sky was almost black. We sustained several hits, but no one hit with shrapnel. Bohlen is a tough target. Good thing we had 10/10 cloud cover.*

NEWSPAPER CLIPPING - (Source unknown)

USSTAF revealed yesterday that 25 bombers and five fighters are missing from Sunday's operations over Berlin. At the same time it announced that photographs taken during the attack showed excellently placed bombs carpeting the centrally located Schlesicher and North Station rail yards and fires burning in the Tempelhof airdrome and marshalling yards. Libs which struck at industrial objectives in the

84

suburban areas also acheived good results,
the photos showed.

End of Clipping

[See notation following clipping of Mar 18 – grh]

==

MARCH 18
BREAKFAST AT 220, BREIFING AT 320. OFF TO BERLIN, GERMANY.
HEAVY AND ACCURATE FLAK. VISUAL TARGET. SAW A LOT OF NICE BIG FIRES AND MANY
BOMB HITS. SHIP HIT BY FLAK IN WINGS AND BALL TURRET. FIGHTERS IN AREA. I SAW A
262 (JET).
MISSION LENGTH 9 HRS.

MISSION #14 COMPLETE.

From the diary of Lt. Marty Raber:

Went to Big B [Berlin – grh] to hit RR yard. Was partly visual but bombing was done by instrument. Bombs hit Templehof
Airdrome & part of marshalling yard. Flak was moderate. Very accurate on other Sqd [squadron – grh] but not ours. Saw
one B 17 go down. 7 chutes came out.

From the diary of Lt. Paul Katz:

Today was the day. I flew no. 12A or 13 as you would say. Besides being 13, it turned out
to be the "Big B" (Berlin). We got to Berlin without any Flak. When we got there it was
visual which means all our Radar jamming devices were no good against there[sic] Flak guns as
they could aim at us visually. They through[sic] up a lot of Flak but we were pretty lucky and
[didn't] get very much of it. We only had two holes in the ship. According to the papers this
was the largest daylight raid on Berlin yet.

"Mission Sheet" of S/Sgt George Odenwaller:

MISSION: #12
TARGET: BERLIN
FLAK: INTENSE, ACCURATE
FIGHTERS: ME 262's JET A/C
DAMAGE: SOME
TAKE-OFF: 08:30

```
E.T.R:           16:30
T.T:             8 HOURS
OXYGEN TIME: 5 HOURS
BOMB LOAD:   10 500 LB. G.P.'s & 2 M-17 CLUSTERS
ALT:             27,000 FT
SHIP No:         636
NAME:            OUTHOUSE MOUSE  OR-N
TEMP:            - 42 F.
```

From the diary of S/Sgt Walter Limberger:

#12
Target – Berlin, Germany
Flak – Intense - Visual
Fighters – Me262 Jets
Damage – Some
Take Off – 0830 hrs
Landed – 1630 hrs
Total Time – 8 hrs
Oxygen – 5 hrs
Bombs – 10-500 lb G. P.'s and 2-M-17's
Altitude – 27,000 ft.
Ship # – 636 Out House Mouse
Temp – -42

The heart of Germany also the Capitol. But we gave it the worst blitz by any Bomb Group
(By Central Intelligence).   The 322Sqd. Got hit by ME262's.   They got it pretty bad.
We were lucky though. Some scared. Berlin visual (no cloud cover). Sure was rough.

From the diary of Lt. Phil Darby:

The "Doc" was not at the hospital. I'll go back day after tomorrow.

[Lt. Darby's ear infection has him in the hospital, so I've temporarily relocated his diary entry to be after those of the other crew members to keep the aircrew mission observations together. - grh]

NEWSPAPER CLIPPING - (Source unknown)

1,300 Heavies Plaster Berlin
Biggest Day

Raid of War
Hits Rails

Berlin, feeling the cold steel of Allied pincers closing tighter every day and stung by RAF Mosquitoes for 26 nights in a row, took its soundest daylight pasting[sic] of the war yesterday when more than 1,300 8th Air Force heavies winged over the Nazi capitol to shower railroad and industrial targets with more than 3,000 tons of high explosives and incendiaries.

It was a 50-ton-a-minute deluge and the 8th's 17th and strongest attack of the war on the city. For more than an hour the heavies roared over, hitting two rail targets in the heart of the city and two war plants in the industrial suburbs.

The rail objectives - the Schleisicher Station traffic center and the North Station freight yards - formed the focal point of the attack, nearly 1,000 Forts pouring their loads on these two targets two miles from the Air Ministry. They had been hit by the bombers in the Feb. 26 attack, until yesterday the largest daylight assault on the city.

Lay Down 1,000 Pounders

The 300 Liberators in the force swung over suburban Tegel and Hennigsdorf to lay down patterns of 1,000-pounders and incendiaries on the sprawling Rheinmetall Borsig plant, which makes guns, bombs and torpedoes, and on the Borsig Lokomotiv works, a factory that covers 120 acres and turns out wide varieties of armored vehicles.

The 700 escorting Mustangs ran into scattered opposition from the Luftwaffe, but none of the enemy planes, some of them jet-propelled Me262s, got in a solid blow against the bombers. At least 13 Nazis were reported shot down.

Some of the 8th's fighters teamed with Red Air Force fighter planes for the first time when they combined with pilots of Soviet Yaks to quell a Luftwaffe strafing attack on a Soviet airfield east of the Oder River.

Run Into German Planes

As Capt. Ralph L. Cox, of Robbstown, Tex, described the fight, the Mustangs peeled off to patrol the Oder River territory, when they ran into four German FW190s diving to attack the airdrome. Cox and fellow pilots tangled

with the raiders as the Soviet pilots rose
to the defense and Cox sent down one
plane in flames while the Yaks drove the
rest of them away.

The heavies, which ran into thick cloud
Saturday while attacking oil, industrial
and communications targets, got a hand
from the weather yesterday when big
breaks in the clouds enabled bombardiers
to pound away visually on most targets.

Saturday's force, which consisted of
1,300 heavies and 750 fighters, hit
synthetic oil plants at Bohlen and
Ruhland, tank factories at Hanover and
the marshalling yards at Munster. Eight
bombers and two fighters failed to return.

WASHINGTON, Mar. 18 (ANS) –
Since Kraut jet-propelled fighter planes
appeared in action last July, four U.S.
bombers and seven fighters have been lost
to their attacks, the War Department
announced today. On the other side of the
picture, 49 enemy jets have been knocked
out of the air by U. S. planes; 55 more
have been destroyed on the ground.

End of Clipping

[Lt. Raber's scrapbook had the above articles as one complete clipping revealing an error in Lt. Harvey's clipping where by mistake he had switched the clipping of Mar 17 for the section beginning "Run Into German Planes". In addition, Lt. Raber's scrapbook also contained the second article date-lined WASHINGTON, Mar. 18 (ANS) and Lt. Harvey did not. – grh]

===

MARCH 19
SQUADRON STAND-DOWN. REGULAR MORNING MEETING. COMMUNICATIONS SCHOOL IN P.M. MEETING OF SQD IN P.M. TO PRESENT MEDALS. I TOO AM A HERO NOW. I GOT MY AIR MEDAL.
WENT TO CAMBRIDGE IN P.M.

From the diary of Lt. Paul Katz:

Squadron standown [sic] *today. No flying. Am up on the list for tomorrows mission.*

Uneventful day. One of the boys (Bill Adams) finished up. We had some drinks at the "Horse and Wagon" pub.

[Presume Bill completed his 35 missions - grh]

===

MARCH 20
STAND-DOWN TO-DAY[sic] DUE TO WEATHER OVER THE CONTINENT. REGULAR MORNING MEETING. FLEW FORMATION AIR TO AIR GUNNERY MISSION OVER CHANNEL. TWO SHIPS IN FORMATION WERE HIT. ONE SHIP LOST AN ENGINE. MORE FUN !
WENT TO U.S.O. SHOW IN EVENING.

[This is an instance where a practice turns deadly. – grh]

From the diary of Lt. Paul Katz:

We are not on the list for today's mission so I guess we will just take it easy. Weather standown [sic].

From the diary of Lt. Phil Darby:

Doc Glorig says I have Otitus Media. I will enter the hospital tomorrow.

===

MARCH 21
LISTED SPARE #3 TODAY SO DID NOT FLY. REGULAR MORNING MEETING. A.F.C.E. TRAINER WORKED ON B-26. [model aircraft he is building. – grh]
FLEW 909 (FAMOUS SHIP FOR NO ABORTS AND MOST EFFECTIVE MISSIONS.) ON SLOW TIME. WENT TO GREAT DUNMOORE (LIMMY FIELD) TO PICK UP A PASSENGER. EVERY ONE[sic] ON THE FIELD TURNED OUT TO WATCH US LAND AND TAKE-OFF. MADE A BEAUTIFUL LANDING. JOKE OF THE WEEK - I BOUNCED LIKE HELL UPON RETURN TO BASSINGBOURN ! WENT TO PICTURES IN P.M. "ANIMAL KINGDOM".

[The "Nine-O-Nine" was the sister ship of the "Out House Mouse" and was maintained by the same ground crew lead by M/Sgt. Rollin L. Davis of Miles, Texas. On April 25, 1945, the "Nine-O-Nine" completed 140 combat missions without a mechanical abort – the best record in the entire 8th Air Force. The "Out House Mouse" completed 139 missions. For this outstanding record M/Sgt. Davis was awarded the Bronze Star with cluster.

The B-17 predates the pressurized crew areas. When in his ball, the ball turret gunner's back pressed directly on the aluminum hatch door and in the narrow tail, the tail gunner's sides pressed against the bare sides of the fuselage, where the air on the outside reached as low as -40 degrees. Normally, their only protection against the cold environment was their oxygen mask which they used when flying above 10,000 feet and their electrically heated flight suits.

George Odenwaller related that when they were trucked out to the "Nine-O-Nine" before dawn, he opened the hatch door on his ball turret, turned on a few lights and found himself looking at a ball turret fully upholstered in old fleece from damaged fleece-lined flight jackets. He called to Lindy, the tail gunner, and he reported that his tail gun position was also fully lined with fleece. After completing the mission and landing, the ground crew asked if everything was okay with their positions. They raved about the cozy cocoons and how much more comfortable they were than just the electrically heated flight suits alone. For their next mission, the ground crew had worked through the night and part of the next day fleece-lining the ball and tail of the "Out House Mouse". To his knowledge, this ground-crew maintained the only two B-17's with upholstered gun positions. – grh]

From the diary of Lt. Paul Katz:

Not on todays list. They seem to be holding our crew back for some reason or other. We only fly about one out of every four missions. That means it will take a long time for me to finish my tour.

From the diary of Lt. Phil Darby:

I'm assigned to ward #40 a convalescence ward. Dick Kubek who has a skin rash is my next door neighbor.

==

MARCH 22
BREAKFAST AT 400, BRIEFING AT 500. OFF TO BOMB GERMAN BARRACKS 2 MILES SOUTH OF DORSTEN. VISUAL TARGET. BOMB LOAD 34-100 LB GENERAL PURPOSE BOMBS. MODERATE BUT DAMNED ACCURATE FLAK. WE WERE HIT IN FUSELAGE AND #1 ENGINE OIL TANK. 2 SHIPS (OTHER GROUP) WENT DOWN OVER TARGET. ONE SHIP BROKE IN HALF. ONE OF OUR SHIPS MISSING. THIS TARGET WAS A REQUEST FROM GEN. "IKE". HAD A FEW FIGHTERS. WE PUT "OUT HOUSE MOUSE" IN FOR ENGINE CHANGE AND GENERAL REPAIRS. 7-1/2 HR MISSION.

MISSION #15 COMPLETE.

PICTURES IN EVENING. "STRIKE UP THE BAND".

From the diary of Lt. Marty Raber:

We went to Dorston at Gen. Ike's request to bomb a command post. We clabbered [sic] the target. Flak was heavy and accurate. We lost a few boys not counting those wounded. The Flak was bursting right under the plane. I saw a B 17 go down & break in half in mid air.

From the diary of Lt. Paul Katz:

Up for a mission today. We raided some military installations near Dorsten. It was a short mission, but the Flak was accurate. We only got two holes in old Outhouse, but some of the other crews weren't that lucky. One ship had to crash land in Belgium injuring some of the crew. We got back without any mishap. Darby is in the hospital with a bad ear as the result of a cold so we are flying with a new Co-Pilot.

"Mission Sheet" of S/Sgt George Odenwaller:

MISSION: #13
TARGET: DORSTEN
FLAK: MODERATE
FIGHTERS: NONE
DAMAGE: SOME
TAKE-OFF: 10:00
E.T.R: 16:30
T.T: 6:30
OXYGEN TIME: 3:00
BOMB LOAD: 10 500 LB. G.P.'s & 2 M-17 CLUSTERS
ALT: 25,000 FT
SHIP No: 636
NAME: OUTHOUSE MOUSE OR-N
TEMP: - 36 F.

From the diary of S/Sgt Walter Limberger:

#13
Target — Dorsten, Ger.
Flak — Moderate
Fighters — None
Damage — Slight Few holes
Take Off — 1000 hrs
Landed — 1630 hrs
Total Time — 6 hrs 30 min
Oxygen — 3 hrs
Bombs — 10-500 lb G. P.'s and 2-M-17 Cluster's
Altitude — 25,000 ft.

Ship # – 636 Out House Mouse

Temp – -36°

As far as I'm concerned, this was rough, as I saw a B-17 go down. ½ way down it broke in half in center fuselage [sic]. No chutes came out and all airmen went in with it. Horrible feeling it gives one. A direct flak hit exploded mid ship of aircraft.

From the diary of Lt. Phil Darby:

Kubek is a great fella. He is Ground Safety Officer at Division Hdqs.[headquarters – grh]. *We play a couple of rubbers* [series of bridge hands - grh] *with Davenport and "Butch". I think Kubek is from Detroit.*

Article from the London Edition of <u>THE STARS AND STRIPES</u> Vol 5 No 120-1d
Friday, March 23, 1945

3,000 Allied Planes Blitz Ruhr, Luftwaffe Airfields

*** *** *** *** **** ***

66-Mi. Smokescreen Hides West
Few Enemy Planes Up, 22 KO'd

Heavy bombers of the 8th Air Force and the RAF again lent their crushing weight yesterday to the great tactical blitz on Nazi military and communications zones in the Ruhr.

More than 1,300 Fortresses and Liberators of the 8th, with a cover of some 700 Mustangs, lashed out in excellent weather at nine Wehrmacht administration and supply centers ringing Essen in the Ruhr and continued to blast enemy airfields, striking four more near Frankfurt-on-Main and Stuttgart and one at Ahlhorn, near Bremen, which had been pommeled[sic] in Wednesday's big blow.

RAF heavies were out in great strength and with strong escorts, indicating the 8th and Bomber Command had well over 3,000 aircraft out. The British heavies threw their punches at three Nazi advance bases for the lower Rhine near Wesel - Bocholt, Dorstein and Dulmen - hit the railway center of Hildesheim, near Hanover, and climaxed the day with a Lancaster-borne assault with 11-ton bombs on railway bridges in northwest Germany.

Thunder Up from Italy

From the south, Forts and Libs of the 15th thundered up from Italy to bomb the Ruhland oil refinery, 70 miles south of Berlin, and oil refineries and railroad yards in Vienna. At Ruland, Libs picked up part of the escort of 8th Mustangs for the bomb run, thus capping a big day for the fighters, too.

The Mustangs had the distinction of providing protection for three separate forces, for in addition to shielding the 8th and 15th, some went along to defend the RAF's Lancasters which poured 11-tonners on the bridges. Some scattered enemy air opposition was met but no passes were made at the heavies and 8th fighters KO'd 13 in the air and shot up nine more in strafing attacks on fields in central Germany.

The 4th Mustang Group, which met the 15th Libs over Ruhland, bagged ten of these planes in a fierce battle with 15 FW190s which had just taken off from an enemy airfield. Lt. Col. Sidney S. Woods, of Somerton, Ariz., who led the group, shot down five for his first kills in the ETO after shifting here from the Pacific.

The specific targets for 8th heavies around Essen were at Bottrop, Gladbeck, Barminghotten, Dorsten, Westerholt, Mulheim, Hinsbeck, Hattingen and Geresheim. Ack-ack over these objectives was particularly heavy but over the four airfields in the Frankfurt and Stuttgart areas - Kitzengen, Giebelstadt, Rhein-Main and Schwabisch-Hall - there was only light opposition.

End of Article

===

MARCH 23
STOOD DOWN AGAIN TODAY. MISSED THE MORNING MEETING. FIRED .45 PISTOL (15 RDS) IN A.M. WITH KITTY [Paul Katz – grh]. HAD A.F.C.E. TRAINER IN P.M. NITE[sic] TRAINING MISSION TONITE[sic] BUT #3 ENGINE FUEL PUMP OUT. MISSION SCRUBBED.

WENT TO PICTURES IN EVENING. "AND NOW TOMORROW".
PLAYED BRIDGE AT NITE[sic].

From the diary of Lt. Paul Katz:

Not on the list for todays [sic] mission so am taking it easy. Tomorrow is a standown [sic] so I will not be flying then either.

From the diary of Lt. Phil Darby:

Today we had a picnic out in a nearby field. There were about five nurses. We had chicken sandwiches and coffee.

==

MARCH 24
GROUPE[sic] FLEW TWO MISSIONS TODAY. SQD FLEW ONE MISSION IN P.M. AND LANDED
AT NITE[sic]. BOMBED AIR FIELD AT HENGENLD, HOLLAND. HIT THE TARGET SMACK IN
THE MIDDLE. FLAK LITE[sic] BUT <u>VERY</u> ACCURATE. LT. SCHILLY FLEW AS CO-PILOT ON HIS
FIRST MISSION.
SHORT MISSION 6 HRS.

MISSION #16 COMPLETE.

From the diary of Lt. Paul Katz:

Today was supposed to be standown [sic] but an M.E. [Maximum Effort i.e. all air worthy aircraft fly – grh] was called and the group flew two missions. I flew in the afternoon mission. It was visual and we bombed an airfield near Hengelo, Holland. We had been over that field before on our way into Germany and never got any Flak but today they must have known we were coming and they really through it up at us. Today was the first time I could see the red in the center of the Flak bursts and that ain't good. We all got back safely though. My pass starts tonight.

94

"Mission Sheet" of S/Sgt George Odenwaller:

MISSION: #14
TARGET: TWENTE / ENSCHEDEN
FLAK: MEAGER
FIGHTERS: NONE
DAMAGE: NONE
TAKE-OFF: 14:00
LANDED: 20:30
T.T: 6:00
OXYGEN TIME: 3:00 30 MIN
BOMB LOAD: 5 500 LB. G.P.'s & 5 M-17 CLUSTERS & LEAFLETS
ALT: 21,000 FT
SHIP No: 623
NAME: NO NAME
TEMP: - 30 F.

From the diary of S/Sgt Walter Limberger:

#14

Target — Twent/Enscheden, Germany

Flak — Meager

Fighters — None

Damage — None

Take Off — 1400 hrs

Landed — 2030 hrs

Total Time — 6 hrs 30 min

Oxygen — 3 hrs 30 min

Bombs — 5-500 lb G. P.'s and 5-M-17 Cluster's

Altitude — 21,000 ft.

Ship # — 623 No Name

Temp — -30°

Nice one today. Only over the front lines ½ hr. Also flak wasn't to [sic] bad. We blitzed
an airfield and hit runways and many buildings. Don't think the Jerries will be able to use it
for a while.

From the diary of Lt. Phil Darby:

Some Kraut prisoners came in today. We have a Corporal with the Iron Cross. He sure is eager to
please. Can hardly blame him. First day on the job.

8th AF Aided Paratroops

Having culminated its role in the Rhine crossing Saturday with blazing bomber and fighter sweeps up and down enemy territory, activities of the 8th Air Force fell off sharply yesterday as approximately 250 Liberators and some 250 Mustangs and Thunderbolts attacked three underground oil storage depots near Brunswick and Hamburg.

But on Saturday, the 8th put together a mighty procession of bombers and fighters which flew 3,000 sorties in cooperation with the troops streaming across the river. The bombers, which had been devastating enemy airfields east of the Rhine for three days, plastered 16 more and dropped weapons and supplies in a daring low-level operation to paratroops immediately after they had landed.

From dawn to dusk Thunderbolts and Mustangs patrolled the battle area, riddling troop concentrations, supply columns, rail yards and airfields. Only 66 Nazi fighters were met, an indication of the results of the bombers' relentless attacks on Luftwaffe fields, and 53 of these were shot down. The 8th lost 22 bombers and four fighters during the day.

Liberators which dropped supplies to the airbourne troops bore the brunt of the losses - 20 out of approximately 240 which followed directly behind transports and gliders and dropped the sky-fighters some 600 tons of weapons and medical supplies form 100 feet. The Libs had to battle through an intense storm of 20-mm anti-aircraft, machine-gun and small weapons fire.

The massive operation of the 8th was split three ways. Early in the morning, around 1,050 Forts and Libs hit 12 airfields east of the Rhine. This was followed by the mission supporting the airbourne troops. Then late in the afternoon 450 heavies struck four additional fields in the Reich, raising to 25 the total of airdromes hit by the 8th in its fierce attack on Nazi fighter bases.

At the day's end the German lines were a shambles, supply lines wrecked, rails torn and twisted, airfields gutted and cratered. Long columns of enemy convoys were set aflame and riddled by fighters. An entire motorized infantry battalion was battered and routed by Mustang pilots who caught the unit as it roared along a highway near Cologne.

Fighter pilots reported shooting up 45 locomotives, 210 rail cars, 300 motor vehicles and 21 barges. Most of these transportation elements were loaded with personnel.

End of clipping

==

MARCH 25
48 HR. PASS BEGAN LAST NITE[sic] 3 HOURS BEFORE WE LANDED. SLEPT LATE TODAY. WROTE LETTERS. SEARCHED COUNTRY SIDE[sic] FOR EGGS - FOUND ONE DOZEN FOR ONLY 5 SHILLINGS. CHEAP ! ONLY $1.00 A DOZEN.

From the diary of Lt. Paul Katz:

On pass but staying on the field.

From the diary of Lt. Phil Darby:

Kubek and I went to Cambridge to a formal Tea. The Major (His Worship) was there with his Robes, Chain of Office and his Mace. I was introduced in a loud booming voice to the people in The Guild Hall.

==

MARCH 26
STILL ON PASS. WORKED ON B-26. SENT TRAVEL PAY INFORMATION TO BIGGS FIELD C.O. FOR NECESSARY PAPERS.
WENT TO CAMBRIDGE IN P.M.

From the diary of Lt. Paul Katz:

Still on pass. Nothing new today. Am up for a mission tomorrow.

From the diary of Lt. Phil Darby:

Our nurse is Helen is really a peach. She has a Boston accent but is from New York. I took penicillin for two days (a shot every three hours). She is gentle with the syringe. Marty brought my mail over. He was sure a welcome sight.

==

MARCH 27
BREAKFAST AT 440, BRIEFING AT 540. OFF TO FULDA, GERMANY.
MISSION SCRUBBED. GEN. PATTON BEAT US TO THE TARGET. HE HAD CAPTURED IT
BEFORE WE GOT OFF THE GROUND.
FLEW AIR TO AIR GUNNERY. LT. WILLIAMS LEAD FORMATION AND WE HAD A "RAT RACE"
COMING HOME. MY RITE[sic] WING NEARLY DRUG IN THE CHANNEL ON A TURN TO THE
RIGHT. WE WERE ONLY 200 FEET OFF THE WATER.
SCRUBB #11

[George Odenwaller related a story that may be from this flight. George told of "The Out House Mouse" being so low, that as he stood in the waist of the aircraft, he watched his ball turret fill with water from the tops of the waves as they crossed the English Channel. – grh]

From the diary of Lt. Paul Katz:

Went to briefing for a mission to Fulda, Germany but it was scrubbed as Patton got there before we could take off.

From the diary of Lt. Phil Darby:

Drank beer in the Officer Club this evening and played bridge at 1/10 cent a point. I lost two shillings. "Doc" Glorig lost a piece of cotton in my nose. It took him 45 minutes to find it, giving me a minor operation in the meantime.

==

MARCH 28
BREAKFAST AT 330, BREIFING AT 400. OFF TO BERLIN, GERMANY.
WE WERE LEAD SQD. FLAK HEAVY AND ACCURATE. FLAK HOLES IN WINGS OF 636.
ASSEMBLED OVER CONTINENT. DUE TO BAD WEATHER WE WERE DIVERTED ON WAY

HOME TO A-55. FIGHTERS IN TARGET AREA. LOST FORMATION IN CLOUDS ON WAY HOME OVER FRANCE. STARTED HOME ALONE AND GOT TO FRENCH COAST WHEN DIVERTED AND LANDED AT MELUN, FRANCE. FLEW AT 800FT. DUE TO WEATHER. SPENT NITE[sic] AT MELUN IN COLD WET TENTS. RAIN AND MUD UP TO HERE ! SAW ALOT OF BOMB DAMAGE DONE BY 9TH A.F. IN MELUN. TOOKOUT TWO BLOCKS OF TOWN TO KNOCK OUT A BRIDGE. A BEAUTIFUL CATHEDRAL WAS IN RUINS. LOGED[sic] A LOT OF INSTRUMENT TIME TODAY. LT. SCHILLY FLEW HIS SECOND MISSION AS CO-PILOT.
8-1/2 HR MISSION.

MISSION #17 COMPLETE

[Note: This mission is not actually "complete" as they have landed at Melun, France not England. While Sgt Odenwaller indicates engine damage may have forced the landing (see his Mission Sheet that follows), Lt. Harvey states that they had reached the French coast when diverted to A-55. Per conversations with Phil Darby, this is most likely an airport map coordinate. While he was not on this mission, he agrees that the two diaries indicate that due to engine problems, they were unable to keep up with the formation and thus "lost the formation in clouds" and had started home alone. When they reached the French coast, Lt. Harvey probably "diverted and landed at Melun, France" as instructed during the mission briefing. Thus, the "Out House Mouse" is alone and on the ground in France. As for the reference to the bomb damage at Melun, the B-17's were from the 8th Air Force so the heavy damage sounds like a dig at the bombing ability of the 9th Air Force.

As mentioned in the introduction to these diaries, Al Kus, the waist gunner, had lost his diary during his return home after the war. However, during a telephone conversation I had with him on July 16, 2001, I obtained his permission to take notes as he told me what he could recall of this forced landing in France.

Al stated that to his recollection, two engines were out and a 3rd engine was feathered. They had already dropped out of the formation and with only the one good engine, were barely flying in the heavy fog. Joe instructed everyone to watch out their closest window for a suitable place to land as he was not able to maintain altitude. After nearly hitting the Eiffel Tower in the zero visibility, the navigator Paul Katz saw something. It appeared to be a small field, but at least it was reasonably flat. Joe flew once around the field and then began his approach. There were a lot of local people on the field waving excitedly at them and they all thought they were getting a big welcome. After landing, they saw that they had actually landed on a small, heavily bombed runway. The locals had all been out on the runway attempting to fill in the bomb craters when the "Out House Mouse" suddenly appeared. They had been attempting to wave them OFF but now that they were on the ground, they shouted angrily at the "crazy Americans" as their wounded B-17 rolled past. Somehow Joe had managed to miss all the holes and they had landed safely. According to the recollections of George and Al, they are at Villa Roche about 20 miles southwest of Paris.

During their forced stay, he and two other crewmembers decided to go see Paris despite the fact that they had no way to change out of their flight gear – something that was quite taboo at that time. They borrowed some bicycles from the local people and took off, but soon discovered that Paris had looked a lot closer from the air than it actually was now that the were on the ground, but Al proudly told me that they did manage to get to Melon.

Somehow while in France, two of the three damaged engines were repaired or replaced and the damaged runway was prepared for the weight of the B-17. Despite the short runway and the lack of full power, Joe somehow managed to get the "Out House Mouse" airborne. Lt. Harvey's diary concludes this mission on March 29.

Marty Raber told me that during his debriefing, he was informed that they had bombed a highly critical heavy water facility. Heavy water was the material the German scientists were planning to use to control their nuclear fission experiments that may have lead them to an atomic bomb. - grh]

99

From the diary of Lt. Paul Katz:

Off to Berlin today. It looked like a pretty good mission for Big B. We had an early E.T.A [estimated time of arrival – grh]. *We got to the Target* [sic] *O.K. Then the Flak started coming up. We were pretty well boxed in. We got out with only three small holes in the wing. We Started* [sic] *for home and were diverted to some field on the continent due to weather. We landed at a field near Melon, which is about twenty miles from Paris. We spent the night there as the weather was still bad. Took off the next morning and Started* [sic] *back. Passed over Paris. It is a very beautiful city from the air. Landed at base O.K. I now have 16 missions.*

[Due to the landing in France, Lt. Katz dates his entry as March 28, 29, 1945 – grh]

"Mission Sheet" of S/Sgt George Odenwaller

MISSION:	#15
TARGET:	SPANDAU / STENDA;
FLAK:	VERY INTENSE & ACCURATE
FIGHTERS:	NONE
DAMAGE:	SOME - 2 ENGINS [sic]
TAKE-OFF:	08:00
E.T.R:	
T.T:	UNKNOWN
OXYGEN TIME: 4 HOURS - 20 MIN.	
BOMB LOAD:	5 500 LB. G.P.'s & 5 M-17 CLUSTERS
ALT:	26,000 FT
SHIP No:	636
NAME:	OUTHOUSE MOUSE OR-N
TEMP:	- 38 F..

   AFTER "BOMBS AWAY", TOTAL CLOUD COVER: LOST 1 ENGIN[sic]; FLEW BLIND THRU[sic] SECONDARY GROUP; IN 10/10 CLOUDS [zero visibility - grh] - LOST ANOTHER ENGIN - SOME LOSSES; BECAME LOST - LET DOWN OR BAIL OUT - STAYED WITH A/C; LET DOWN, ALMOST HIT EIFFEL TOWER IN FOG; WAS ALSO ALMOST BROADSIDED BY AN L-3 GRASSHOPPER [a small plane similar to today's Piper Cub - grh] - NAVIGATOR FOUND A SMALL FIELD SOUTH OF PARIS, NAMED VILLA/ROCHE: WE LET DOWN THRU FOG MADE A BUMPY LANDING - WAVED AWAY BY FRENCH WORKMEN. WHEN STOPPED WE WERE TOLD THE RUNWAY WAS BOMBED OUT; THEY WERE MAKING REPAIRS - WE SOMEHOW MISSED ALL THE HOLES - STAYED WITH A/C - REPAIRED 2 DAYS LATER. WHILE ON GROUND, KUS & I TOOK OUR CHANCE TO BIKE TO PARIS WITH FLYING GEAR ON - NOT PICKED UP BY MP's - LUCKY. (PARIS 20 MILES). UPON RETURN TO BASSINGBOURN, FOUND WE WERE M.I.A. - PERSONAL LOCKER CLEANED OUT, INCLUDING SCOTCH, A-2 JACKET, UNIFORMES [sic], EVERYTHING - ALSO GEN'L IKE PICTURE FROM B-17

NOSE DAMAGED BY RUNAWAY PROP. - (A/C No 297061 LL B) 401st SQ. NAME OF A/C "GEN. IKE". NEVER MADE IT TO PARIS !

[S/Sgt. Odenwaller is referring to another famous B-17 named in honor of the famous General and personally christened by him during his visit to Bassingbourn in April 1944. On its 65th mission, a wind-milling No.3 engine propeller sheared off and sliced into the fuselage. Due to the famous namesake of the aircraft, the incident received a lot of attention by the press.

Regarding the lockers, I have been told that to maintain morale, the personal affects and sometimes whole bunks and foot-lockers of airmen who did not return from a mission were immediately removed so that the men who bunked right beside them did not get brooding over the sight of an empty bunk. – grh]

From the diary of S/Sgt Walter Limberger:

#15
Target – Spandau/Berlin, Germany
Flak – Intense
Fighters – None
Damage – Slight Several holes
Take Off – 0800 hrs
Landed – Landed in France – ETR would have been 1500
Total Time –
Oxygen – 4 hrs 20 min
Bombs – 5-500 lb G. P.'s and 5-M-17 Incendiary's
Altitude – 26,000 ft.
Ship # – 636 Out House Mouse
Temp – -38°

We had to make a landing in France. Thought the whole 1st Air division was diverted to landings on the Continent because of weather at Bassingbourne. We had a good time there. The base was a troop carrier base named Villa La Roche. Mission was another rough one.

From the diary of Lt. Phil Darby:

Spent the day reading and writing some letters. There was a movie in the ward. "And Now Tomorrow", with Alan Ladd and Loretta Young.

NEWSPAPER CLIPPING - (Source unknown)

900 Heavies Hit Berlin, Hanover Plants

The 8th Air Force aimed twin blows yesterday at Germany's inner circle of war industry and what may be its last remaining industrial trump card when over 400 Fortresses bombed war plants in suburban Berlin and more than 500 ranged over Hanover to hit factories and railroad marshalling yards.

Significantly, ack-ack gunners in Berlin and Hanover yesterday threw up a stiff umbrella of flak, indicating that the Nazis, in expectation of savage attacks yet to come, may not yet have stripped their vital industries in central Germany.

Some fliers over Berlin, where tank, armored vehicle and weapons factories were attacked, reported particularly heavy barrages of ack-ack fire, besides thick clouds, which made bombing by instrument necessary in most cases. Clouds also covered Hanover, where the targets included plants making half-tracks and other armored vehicles.

Some 350 Mustangs shielded the bombers yesterday, but ran into no enemy fighters, a further gauge of the effectiveness of the 8th's and the 15th Air Force's recent saturation assaults on German airfields and plane factories.

Attacks on oil objectives were carried on yesterday by medium bombers of the 9th Air Force, which flew deep into the Reich to strike oil stores southeast of Paderborn and east of Wurzburg. Fighter-bomber pilots reported a general eastward movement of German transport.

End of Clipping

==

MARCH 29
UP AT 8 A.M. HAD BREAKFAST. WENT TO PREFLIGHT[sic] AND GAS SHIP. (STILL IN FRANCE) WING ADVISED US TO WAIT TIL P.M. FOR TAKE-OFF. TOOK OFF AT 1315. FLEW OVER PARIS AT 1500 FT. BIG PLACE THAT. WE WERE 30 MILES SOUTH OF PARIS, AT MELUN. MADE INSTRUMENT LET-DOWN UPON RETURN HOME. FIND NOW THE GROUPE RETURNED TO BASE LAST NITE[sic]. CHANGE OF ORDERS. LOTS OF RUMORS ABOUT US FAILING TO RETURN.

WENT TO PICTURES IN EVENING WITH TOMMY. GOT 7 LETTERS FROM MARIBELLE UPON RETURN FROM FRANCE.

GROUP STAND DOWN TO-DAY

[While no information is available, it appears that Lt. Harvey may have somehow contacted Bassingbourn for instructions. – grh]

From the diary of Lt. Phil Darby:

Kubek and I drank beer in the Club and played a few games of ping pong. A nurse I call "Lynchy" played me a game then the three of us sat around and talked the rest of the evening. I walked her to her hut.

==

MARCH 30
STOOD DOWN AGAIN TODAY. WENT MORNING MEETING. FLEW PRACTICE MICKY MISSION IN A.M. [a "Micky Mission" is bombing by radar - grh]. WENT TO AFCE [Automatic Flight Control Equipment i.e. autopilot. – grh] IN P.M. FLEW A SLO-TIME SHIP IN EVENING. EVENING SPENT WRITTING LETTERS.

From the diary of Lt. Marty Raber:

We went to Bremen to bomb dock installations. The bombing was good despite the cloud coverage. The Flak was light & accurate. Saw an enemy Fighter attack a lone B 17 in front of us. P51's got right on him. The B17 was O.K. Coming back we had to separate cause of the soup over the channel.

[This is Lt Raber's last diary entry and once again he is obviously flying as lead bombardier with another crew. On the back side of the last page of his diary is the following:
1.   Check Bomb doors.
2.   "   "   Switches (Bombay)
3.   Check Fuses
4.   Pull Pins

From this, I visualize that in the still dark, early hours of a cold damp English morning, a twenty something young man ducks under the open bomb bay doors of an olive drab B-17. Then, pulling a small green notepad out of one of his flight suit pockets, he opens the back cover and once again carefully checks to be SURE he performs those four important steps. – grh]

From the diary of Lt. Paul Katz:

Not up for mission today.

From the diary of Lt. Phil Darby:

Today I come home. The "Doc" says I'm okay, but I kinda hate to leave. I had a swell time. Kubek is really a good friend now. Claude Wright was a Univ. of Neb. student. We have a lot of mutual acquaintances.

==

MARCH 31
BREAKFAST AT 200, BRIEFING AT 300. OFF TO MERSEBURG, GERMANY.
SAW FLAK BUT NO FIGHTERS. BAD WEATHER OVER TARGET WHICH, ALONG WITH POOR
LEADER SHIP, ALMOST COST A LOT OF LIVES. TWO SQD RUN TOGETHER. WE WERE ON
BOMB RUN AND A GROUP COMING OFF TARGET RAN THRU US. THANK GOD IT WAS
OVERCAST TARGET AND NO FIGHTERS HIT US. SHIPS ALL OVER THE SKY. BOMBED
TARGET OF OPPORTUNITY. ALL IN ALL MISSION SNAFU. I'M IN THE "PAY DIRT" NOW AND
THE HOME STRETCH AND ALL THE WAY DOWN HILL. OH, HAPPY ME.
MISSION 9-1/2 HRS LONG

MISSION #18 COMPLETE

["I'm in the 'Pay Dirt' now" refers to Lt. Harvey having completed half of his tour of 35 combat missions. For those civilian readers, SNAFU is military jargon for "Situation Normal – All Fowled Up". A target of opportunity is anything useful to the German war effort - airfields, trains, road intersections, etc. The objective is to expend your bomb load on some useful target rather than to have to drop them uselessly in the English Channel on the way home - grh]

From the diary of Lt. Paul Katz:

Up for number seventeen today. We were briefed to raid the Luna Oil works at Mersberg.
Just mentioning the name of that place is enough to scare every one on the field. It is one of [the]
most heavily guarded targets in Germany [and known for its' heavy flak gun defenses – grh]. *We got*
off O.K. and went in over France. We hit our I.P. without any opposition and started our
bomb run. That was when the fun started. Our Squadron leader had his headup and locked
[i.e. he wasn't thinking and didn't want to hear about it eithter! – grh] . *We went down the run on a*
separate course. There were clouds in our path but he didn't want to climb over them. In the
clouds, another formation coming off the target ran into us. There was nothing but confusion all
over the place. Everybody trying to get out of the way. On top of that, we were in the clouds and
couldn't see anything but shadows of B-17s. Then the Germans started sending the Flak up.
I thought we had it today. We managed to get out of the mess and seven of the ships got back

104

into formation again. We still hadn't dropped our bombs so went around looking for a target. We finally found a town and dropped on it. Got back to base O.K. Next mission puts me over the hump.

"Mission Sheet" of S/Sgt George Odenwaller

MISSION: #16
TARGET: HALLE / ASCHERSLEBEN
FLAK: MODERATE
FIGHTERS: NONE
DAMAGE: NONE
TAKE-OFF: 05:45
LANDED: 14:45
T.T: 9:00
OXYGEN TIME: 5:00
BOMB LOAD: 20 300 LB. BOMBS
ALT: 22,000 FT
SHIP No: 636
NAME: OUTHOUSE MOUSE OR-N
TEMP: - 40 F..

JUST ANOTHER MISSION EXCEPT, AS WE WERE ON OUR BOMB RUN WITH BOMB DOORS OPEN, ANOTHER GROUP, THE 398th B.G. OUT OF NUTHAMSTEAD, WHICH JUST DROPPED IT'S BOMBS, CAME OFF THEIR BOMB DROP & WENT INTO THEIR 360 TURN OFF TARGET & RIGHT INTO OUR FORMATION ABOUT TO DROP. B-17's SIDEWAYS, CLIMBING, DIVING: EVERY WHICH WAY TO AVOID A MID-AIR COLLISION. WE GOT SEPERATED [sic] FROM THE GROUP, SO, SALVOED OUR BOMBS ON SOME SMALL RAILYARD ! CAME HOME ALONE !

From the diary of S/Sgt Walter Limberger:

#16
Target — Aschersleben, Ger.
Flak — Moderate
Fighters — None
Damage — None
Take Off — 05:45 hrs
Landed — 1445 hrs
Total Time — 9 hrs
Oxygen — 5 hrs
Bombs — 20-300 lb
Altitude — 22,000 ft.
Ship # — 636 Out House Mouse
Temp — -40°

This mission itself wasn't too bad but just over the target on our bomb run, another formation that had just dropped their bombs coming off their turn nearly crashed into us as we were at the same altitude. For a while B-17's were going in all directions to avoid mid-air collisions. We were seperated [sic] *from our formation and dropped our bombs on a target of opportunity.*

The reason for all the confusion, visibility was almost zero because of heavy mist and fog in the freezing temperature.

From the diary of Lt. Phil Darby:

Back in the harness again. We went into Cambridge tonight. I think maybe I got a little bit stewed at the "Eagle". However, I met a nice girl at the Dorothy Dance Hall. Have a date for Monday night.

NEWSPAPER CLIPPING - (Source unknown)

Month for 8th

Heavy bombers of the 8th Air Force were idle yesterday after rounding out their greatest month of the war on Saturday, when more than 1,300 Fortresses and Liberators, protected by 850 Mustangs and Thunderbolts, attacked rail, industrial and oil targets in Germany.

During March, featured by the mighty assault that helped clear the way for the Rhine crossings, the 8th unloaded 73,000 tons of bombs on the Reich, surpassing by 15,000 tons its previous heaviest month, June of last year, when its planes dented the French coast in co-operation with the invading Allied forces.

The heavies flew more than 28,500 sorties, bettering by 2,600 the number flown during D-Day month, until now the record month. Fighters made 16,400 sorties, topped only by June, July and August of last year.

The record tonnage represents nearly two tons of bombs dropped every minute during the month. It took the 8th 18 months, from mid-August, 1942, to mid-February, 1944, to drop its first 73,000 tons on Nazi strong points.

The 8th lost 138 bombers and 99 fighters during March, or one plane lost for every 200 sent out. At the same time, 410 enemy fighters were destroyed, 250 shot down and 129 destroyed on the ground by fighters and 31 shot down by bomber gunners.

End of Clipping

===

APRIL 1
WENT TO CHURCH AND COMMUNION TODAY. CAMBRIDGE MY OBJECTIVE IN P.M. FOR PICTURES. GROUPE STAND DOWN TODAY.

From the diary of Lt. Phil Darby:

Not much doing. I slept most of the day. Read "A Yank at Oxford". Good yarn.

From the diary of Lt. Paul Katz:

Stood down today, no flying.

===

APRIL 2
GROUPE [sic] STAND DOWN AGAIN. WORKED ON B-26 MOST OF THE DAY [model - grh]. U.S.O SHOW IN EVENING. GOT PAID TODAY AND STILL HAVE MOST OF IT. MOST AMAZING !

From the diary of Lt. Phil Darby:

I really don't want to meet this gal, but I guess I promised her. I met my little P-51 friend down town. We had a few drinks. I had a very nice date with a blonde from Liverpool. Her name was Mary - the most beautiful girl I've met in England. A Sgt. named Roy was with her friend. We had eggs and chips at a Greek restaurant later. Bill tucker and I had some grog at the Eagle. Oh yes, the woman didn't meet me at the Red Lion.

From the diary of Lt. Paul Katz:

Stood down again today.

===

APRIL 3
SQD. STAND DOWN TODAY. FLEW RUNWAY LOCALIZER WITH CAPT. WARD. FLEW NITE
CROSS COUNTRY WITH LT. SCHILLY. GOT TO BED AT 2400 HRS.

From the diary of Lt. Phil Darby:

A flight today - just flew around and buzzed Cambridge. It was too cloudy to drop blue bombs.

From the diary of Lt. Paul Katz:

Still stood down.

[Entry dated April 3, 4, 1945 – grh]
===

APRIL 4
STAND DOWN AGAIN. FLEW BLUE BOMB MISSION (LT. PITTS) BUT DROPPED NONE DUE TO
LOW CEILINGS. BUZZED CAMBRIDGE ON WAY HOME. CAMBRIDGE AND PICTURES IN
EVENING. "CONSTANT NYMPH".

From the diary of Lt. Phil Darby:

Another stand down. I am officially on flying status again.

===

APRIL 5
BREAKFAST AT 230, BRIEFING AT 330. OFF TO GRAFENWOHR, GERMANY. MADE
INSTRUMENT TAKEOFF AND CLIMBED TO ALTITUDE ON INSTRUMENTS. MUCH BAD
WEATHER. ASSEMBLED OVER CONTINENT. BOMBED ORDANANCE PLANT AND CITY.
BOMB LOAD 34-150 G.P. [general purpose - grh] PLUS 2-M17 INCD. BOMBS [incendiary bombs - grh].
NO FLAK OR FIGHTERS. 10 HR MISSION.

MISSION #19 COMPLETE

From the diary of Lt. Phil Darby:

Mission #11

Long mission to Grafenwehr. Was uneventful. I'm glad because I haven't flown for so long. No flak. We were "D" channel guards.

[Per Phil Darby, "channel guards" were aircraft assigned to monitor given radio channels. Radioman S/Sgt Milton Lloyd must have had an unusually active mission. - grh]

From the diary of Lt. Paul Katz:

Went over the hump today. [mission number 18 for Lt. Katz – grh]. *It was another low altitude mission. It was an ordinance depot near Bayreuth. It was a good mission. No Flak, no fighters.*

From the diary of S/Sgt Niel Jorgenson:

Tenth Mission

Target - Grafenwohr, Germany

Flak - Far off
Fighters - P-51 escourt

Damage - None

Altitude - 15,000. Flew over Paris. 10 Hr miss[ion]
Troubles Encountered - Run away prop was okayed

Ships Name - "Out House Mouse"

"Mission Sheet" of S/Sgt George Odenwaller:

MISSION:	*#17*
TARGET:	*GRAFENWOHR*
FLAK:	*LIGHT*
FIGHTERS:	*AROUND US - 262's & 163's*
DAMAGE:	*NONE*
TAKE-OFF:	*6:10*
LANDED	*16:15*
T.T:	*10 HOURS - 5 MIN*
OXYGEN TIME:	*3 HOURS - 30 MIN.*
BOMB LOAD:	*38 150 LB. G.P.'s & 4 M-17 CLUSTERS*
ALT:	*18,000 FT*
SHIP No:	*636*
NAME:	*OUTHOUSE MOUSE OR-N*
TEMP:	*- 19 F..*

A GOOD MISSION - VERY LONG - BANDITS IN THE AREA - OTHER BOMB GROUPS HIT BY THEM QUITE HEAVILY - BAD WEATHER BUT HIT OUR TARGET ON THE NOSE !

From the diary of S/Sgt Walter Limberger:

#17

Target – Frafenwohr, Ger.

Flak – None

Fighters – None

Damage – None

Take Off – 0610 hrs

Landed – [16:15 – grh]

Total Time – 10 hrs 5 min

Oxygen – 3 hrs 30 min

Bombs – 34-150 lb 2-M-17 Cluster

Altitude – 18,000 ft.

Ship # – 636 Out House Mouse

Temp – -19°

Very easy mission but very long. No flak, but there were some enemy fighters that hit other groups. We were spared again. Weather was poor, but we managed to drop our bombs through 10/10's cover and hit it hard.

NEWSPAPER CLIPPING - (Source unknown)

1,200 Heavies Hit Reich After 1-Day Nazi Air Bid

The flaming air war which the Luftwaffe rekindled Saturday appeared yesterday to have been extinguished one more by U.S. fighters and bomber gunners as over 1,200 Fortresses and Liberators, protected by approximately 750 fighters, bombed rail yards, airfields and oil targets in central Germany without opposition from enemy planes.

The only air activity along the route of the bombers came in the form of three training planes, which were promptly shot down by fighters. On Saturday, when the Luftwaffe daringly attacked a force of 1,300 heavies in strong groups, fighters of the 8th downed 64 planes while bomber gunners accounted for 40, making a grand total of 104.

It was the strongest opposition thrown at the bombers since Mar. 2, when fighters and gunners knocked down 73 planes. The renewal of opposition Saturday cost the 8th 22 bombers and three fighters. Ten bombers and one fighter are missing from yesterday's missions.

End of Clipping

===

APRIL 6
REGULAR MORNING MEETING. NO FLYING TODAY. WORKED ON B-26

CAPT. REID THREATENED TO MAKE ME A CO-PILOT FOR TELLING HIM WHAT I THOUGHT OF TWO OF HIS LEAD PILOTS. BROWN AND SCHOFIELD TWO OF THE VERY WORST !

EARLY TO BED.

[Capt. Reid – probably Capt. William Reid, who I believe was the Operations Officer of the 323rd – grh]

From the diary of Lt. Phil Darby:

Haven't done a thing today except write a couple of letters.

From the diary of Lt. Paul Katz:

Weather standown [sic] *today. No Flying* [sic] *.*

===

APRIL 7
BREAKFAST AT 200, BRIEFING AT 300. OFF TO KOHLENBISSON, GERMANY.
AN AIRFIELD N.E. OF HANOVER. BOMB LOAD 38-150LB. BOMBS. NO FLAK. FIGHTERS WERE IN AREA. OUR LITTLE FRIENDS (ESCORT) SHOT DOWN 63 ENEMY FIGHTERS. LEAD SQD BOMBED WRONG TARGET. HIGH AND LOW SQD HIT PRIMARY TARGET SMACK ON THE HEAD. VISUAL TARGET.

TAKE OFF TIME WAS SET BACK 3 TIMES FOR A TOTAL OF 4 HOURS DELAY. CLIMB THRU[sic] OVERCAST AND INSTRUMENT LET-DOWN. MISSION 8-1/2 HRS. LENGTH.

MISSION #20 COMPLETE.

From the diary of Lt. Phil Darby:

111

Mission #12
Up at 0100 this A.M. We took off at 1005. The mission was to Kohlenbisson; an airfield. There were bandits in the area but we didn't see them. No flak (we skirted the area). We flew No.2 in the diamond. Carried a load of 38-150lb bombs.

[The diamond is a 4-aircraft formation vs. the usual 3-aircraft No.2 is the wingman. – grh]

From the diary of Lt. Paul Katz:

Flew number 19, today. It was another low altitude mission. We bombed an airfield near Hannover. It was really a milk run. I think it was the easiest one yet. I hope the rest of them are the same. Only six more to go to make 1st Lt.

From the diary of S/Sgt Niel Jorgenson:

Eleventh Mission

Target - Koelenbissen, Germany

Flak - Very Light
Fighters - P-51's Spitfires escourt

Damage - None

Altitude - 15,000.   8 Hr miss[ion]
Troubles Encountered - None

Ships Name - "Out House Mouse"

"Mission Sheet" of S/Sgt George Odenwaller:

MISSION:	*#18*
TARGET:	*KOHLENBISSEN*
FLAK:	*LIGHT*
FIGHTERS:	*IN AREA*
DAMAGE:	*NONE*
TAKE-OFF:	*11:30*
LANDED:	*18:30*
T.T.:	*7 HOURS*
OXYGEN TIME:	*3 HOURS - 30 MIN.*
BOMB LOAD:	*38 150 LB. G.P.'s & 2 M-17 CLUSTERS*
ALT:	*15,000 FT*
SHIP No:	*636*
NAME:	*OUTHOUSE MOUSE OR-N*
TEMP:	*- 19 F..*

WE WENT OVER THE "HUMP" THIS TIME - FIGHTERS IN THE AREA - P-51's KNOCKED DOWN 53 GERMAN A/C - ME-262's, FW-190's: BOMBER GUNNERS GOT ANOTHER 35. WE COULD SEE THE FIGHTERS OUT THERE BUT WERE NOT ATTACKED BY THEM - TOO BUSY WITH OUR 51's AND 47's!

["51's AND 47's" refer to our P-51 and P-47 fighters.   S/Sgts Odenwaller and Limberger are over the "hump" because they now have completed half their required mission count of 35 missions. - grh]

From the diary of S/Sgt Walter Limberger:

 # [18 – grh]

Target – Kohlenbissen, Ger.

Flak – Light to moderate

Fighters – Some in area

Damage – None

Take Off – 1130 hrs

Landed – 1830 hrs

Total Time – 7 hrs

Oxygen – 3-1/2 hrs

Bombs – 38-150 lb G. P.'s and 2-M-17 Incendiary Cluster's

Altitude – 15,000 ft.

Ship # – 636 Out House Mouse

Temp – -19°

A good mission. Fighters over the target area but didn't see any. According to 8th Air Force H.Q., P-51's shot down 63 ME262's. Also air gunners got an estimated 40 more. Am going down hill, as its said, towards finishing my missions.

[Number 18 for S/Sgt Limberger – grh]

NEWSPAPER CLIPPING - (Source unknown)

Visual Bombing Over Targets

The bombers had ideal weather yesterday, with visual bombing prevailing over all targets except a rail yard at Plauen, 40 miles southwest of Chemnitz. The target area stretched from just west of Berlin to 15 miles south of Nuremberg.

Three airfields were hit, one southwest of Dessau and the others southwest and south of Nuremberg. Rail yards beside those at Plauen were at Stendal, 70 miles west of

Berlin; at Hof, 15 miles southwest of Plauen; and at Eger, 30 miles southeast of Plauen.

Ordinance depots in the Bayreuth area, 40 miles northeast of Nuremberg, were pounded and another objective in the Nuremberg area was a jet-propelled repair plant at Furth, north of the city. Fifty-five miles west of Berlin, the bombers hit an oil depot at Derben.

Flak, described as meager by airmen, represented the only opposition for the day. One fighter pilot called it a quiet day everywhere in enemy territory, with "not a thing moving."

Heavy bombers of the 15th Air Force made their third consecutive raid on the Brenner Pass route yesterday, besides plastering railroad bridges along the northern Italy front.

End of Clipping

===

APRIL 8

SLEPT LATE (UNTIL 1200 TO BE EXACT). PUT MY ENGINEER IN FOR PROMOTION TO S/SGT. SUBMITTED MY PREFERANCE FOR INSTRUCTOR IN ZONE OF INTERRIOR AFTER MISSIONS COMPLETE. [Zone of Interior is continental U.S.-grh]. WORKED ON B-26 IN EVENING WENT TO BALDOCK. HAD A VERY NICE MEAL AT THE "GEORGE AND DRAGON" HOTEL. IN BED AT 1200 MIDNITE[sic].

[Lt. Harvey's engineer is S/Sgt Niel Jorgenson – grh]

From the diary of Lt. Phil Darby:

Went into Baldock on the train with Miller, Harvey and Katz. Stayed at a Hotel Bar all evening and had fried chicken in the dining room.

From the diary of Lt. Paul Katz:

Not on the list to fly today so just taking it easy. Today is your birthday darling. Happy Birthday. I hope we never have to spend another one away from each other.

===

APRIL 9
REGULAR MORNING MEETING. AIR-CRAFT REC [sic] IN A.M. FLEW A CAMERA MISSION
(BOMBING) IN EVENING. LANDED A 1930 HRS.

PICTURES AT NITE "DANCE IN MANHATTEN". WROTE LETTERS AND EARLY TO THE SACK.
GOT FLAK OVER COVINGTON, ENG. WHILE ON CAMERA MISSION.

["air-craft rec" refers to aircraft recognition training. – grh]

From the diary of Lt. Phil Darby:

Regular Sqd stand down day [sic]. *We flew a camera bombing mission in the P.M. They shot at us over Coventry. One red burst.*

From the diary of Lt. Paul Katz:

Squadron standown [sic]. *No Flying.*

===

APRIL 10
BREAKFAST AT 630, BRIEFING AT 730. OFF TO ORANIENBURG, GERMANY.
BOMBED AN ORDANANCE PLANT. MY WHAT A LOT OF SMOKE AND BIG FIRES. BOMB
LOAD WAS DELAY (6 BOMBS 500#), 2, 4, 6, 12, 24, 72 HOURS. PLUS 2 M17'S INCINDERARY. NO
FLAK OVER TARGET (USUALLY A VERY HEAVY FLAK TARGET) BUT IN STEAD[sic] ENEMY
FIGHTERS HIT THE DIVISION. TWO B-17'S WERE SHOT DOWN OVER TARGET. NO CHUTES
CAME OUT. BOTH SHIP'S WERE ON FIRE AND BROKE UP. SAW A B-17 GET A DIRECT HIT OF
FLAK. IT EXPLODED AND I WATCHED IT TO THE GROUND BUT NO CHUTES CAME OUT. NO
DOUBT ALL WERE KILLED WHEN HIT. MISSION A SUCCESS. WE PUT MISSION NO. 101 ON
636 WITH OUT[sic] ABORT. TARGET WAS 30 MILES NORTH OF BERLIN. LENGTH OF MISSION
8-1/2 HRS.

MISSION #21 COMPLETE

[This mission is most likely one of the reasons my father could not talk of his experiences in the war.
Nightmares plagued him all of his life and he would often yell out to the unseen men in his sleep to "bail-out!"

The aircrews flew three missions and then "stood-down" during the fourth mission. The aircraft however
would often be used by other crews when their own assigned aircraft is unavailable, usually undergoing
repairs. Thus, as Lt. Harvey noted, while this is his 21st mission, it is mission #101 without an abort for 636
("Out House Mouse") which flew a total of 139 consecutive combat missions without an abort. Her sister
ship, the "Nine-O-Nine", flew 140 missions. These remarkable records are the first and second best records
of the entire Eighth Air Force. At Bassingbourn, these two aircraft were parked beside one another on
hardstand #3 and #4 and maintained by the same ground crew lead by MSgt. Rollin L. Davis. – grh]

From the diary of Lt. Phil Darby:

Mission #13
We bombed Oranianberg about ten miles north of Berlin. There was no flak, but ME262 Jet planes came up to intercept us. A B-17 was hit by flak over Whittenberge. It burst into flames, then the bombs exploded. The plane spiraled slowly down (in about 3 pieces) a huge sheet of flame. It is such a pathetic and helpless sight. None got out. We carried delayed action bombs.

From the diary of Lt. Paul Katz:

Up for number 20 today. We bombed a munitions depot at Pranienberg which is a suburb of Berlin. Nothing much happened on the way in. Coming off the target we were hit by fighters. Our group didn't get it too bad. One ship had its controls shot away. The groups behind us caught hell though and lost quite a few ships. A group coming to the target in front of us caught some Flak over Wettenberg. I saw one ship get a direct hit. It caught fire and then exploded. I watched it go down. It was the first ship I've seen go down and I hope it is the last. It was horrible. They didn't have a chance.

From the diary of S/Sgt Niel Jorgenson:

12th Mission

Target - Oranienburg, Germany

Flak - Light but accurate
Fighters - 10 grps [groups - grh] Fighter support. ME-262 & ME-410's

Damage - None

Altitude - 25,000 Ft.

Troubles Encountered - None

Ships Name - "Out House Mouse"

"Mission Sheet" of S/Sgt George Odenwaller:

MISSION: *#19*
TARGET: *ORANIENBURG / LO RECHLIN / LARZ*
FLAK: *NONE*
FIGHTERS: *PLENTY - ME 210's & FW 190's*

```
DAMAGE:        NONE
TAKE-OFF:      08:30
LANDED:        17:00
T.T:            9 HOURS
OXYGEN TIME: 4 HOURS - 30 MIN.
BOMB LOAD:   5  500 LB. G.P.'s & 5 M-17 CLUSTERS
ALT:           28,000 FT
SHIP No:       636
NAME:          OUTHOUSE MOUSE  OR-N
TEMP:          - 29 F.
```

From the diary of S/Sgt Walter Limberger:

#19

Target — Oranianburg, Ger.

Flak — None

Fighters — Plenty

Damage — None

Take Off — 0800

Landed — 1700 hrs

Total Time — 9 hrs

Oxygen — 4-1/2 hrs

Bombs — 5-500 lb G. P.'s and 5-M-17's

Ship # — 636 Out House Mouse

Temp — -29

Mission today was rough. ME262's got 38 17's (from all groups). I saw 2 go down in flames from flak, fighters [took] another one. Saw only a few bail out, terrible feeling. 262's came in on our tail. I fired many rounds to no avail. Many prayers said today as always.

NEWSPAPER CLIPPING - (Source unknown)

8th Fighters Bag Record 245
Jet Bases
Hit Again
By Heavies

The battered Luftwaffe reeled from yet another U.S. blow yesterday as more than 1,300 Fortresses and Liberators and 850 fighters of the 8th Air Force pounded seven jet fighter bases within an arc swinging north, west and south 70 miles from Berlin.

Strong groups of Nazi jets got off the ground to battle, but the U.S. fighters knocked down 18 and roared through to destroy 227 more planes on the ground to establish a new record for fighters of the 8th, whose best day previously had been Sept. 5 of last year, when 177 were destroyed in the air and on the ground.

The 339th Mustang Group also set a new fighter record for the 8th by destroying 100 planes on the ground to surpass the record 70 set by the 56th Thunderbolt Group on last September's record day. One bomber group battled 40 to 50 jets for nearly an hour, but most groups were hit only once or twice before fighters and gunners drove them off.

Clear Weather Prevails

The destruction boosted the 8th's two-day toll of Luftwaffe ships to 329, of which 310 were KO'd on landing strips. Since Saturday, when fighters and bomber gunners shot down 104, the Luftwaffe has lost 437 planes through U.S. action.

It was the eighth straight day the 8th has been operational and the fourth day running it has dispatched upwards of 1,000 bombers. Clear weather again prevailed over the Continent and bombing was visual over all targets.

The attacks brought to 27 the total number of jet airfields in the Reich hit during the last seven days. The seven strips in the Berlin arc, running from the northernmost point, were at Larz, near Lake Muritz; Parchin, just west of the lake; Neuruppin, 40 miles northwest of Berlin; Oranienburg, 18 miles north of the capitol; Briest, near Brandenburg, west of Berlin; Burg, close to Magdeburg; and Zerbst, southwest of Berlin, adjacent to Dessau.

Destroy 83 Nazi Planes

In addition to the assault on the fields, the bombers and fighters struck at a jet experimental field at Rechlin, also in the Lake Muritz area and called the "Wright Field" of Germany, and hit an ordnance depot at Oranienburg.

Full reports turned in by 8th Air Force airmen who blistered ten airfields near Munich Monday and destroyed 83 Nazi planes on the ground, indicated that the Luftwaffe has been driven from its fields and now uses auto highways for air strips, dispersing its planes in wooded areas along the roads to escape detection.

   Most of the planes destroyed were found parked in or near highways south of Munich. Crews were working on some of the planes, which were camouflaged with branches, and one pilot saw nearly 100 ships parked on what appeared to be a farm. The same flier also saw dozens of shining, new JU88s lying under trees beside one roadway and managed to shoot up two of them.

   End of Clipping

===

APRIL 11
BREAKFAST AT 530, BRIEFING AT 630. OFF TO FRIEBURG, GERMANY, (9 MILES SOUTH OF CENTER OF MUNICH).
BOMBED UNDERGROUND OIL PLANT. BOMB LOAD 6-1000 LBS.
NO FIGHTERS BUT GOT FLAK TURNING OFF TARGET FROM MUNICH. FLAK MODERATE AND ACCURATE. BEGAN MISSION AS SPARE SHIP. AT ASSEMBLY WE MOVED INTO #3 POSITION ON 4TH ELEMENT. ENDED UP LEADING FOURTH ELEMENT FROM FRONT LINES IN TO TARGET AND HOME. ONE SHIP ABORTED AND ONE CAME HOME ON TWO ENGINES. MISSION WAS 9 HRS. LONG.

MISSION #22 COMPLETE.

JUST TO NITE[sic] OUR 48 HR. PASS WAS SCRUBBED UNTIL FRIDAY SINCE ONE CREW HAS NOT GOTTEN HOME FROM MISSION YET.

From the diary of Lt. Phil Darby:

Mission #14
Bombed an oil depot three miles west of Munich with a load of 5-1000 pounders. Landed with about 40 gals of gas in each tank. [That is possibly only 15-20 minutes of flying time for a B-17 – grh] Recvd [received - grh] some flak on the starboard side after leaving the target. Saw the Alps (covered with snow). Also flew over Lake Constance on Swiss frontier. Assembly was over Paris. Bomb run up Danube River.

From the diary of Lt. Paul Katz:

Number 11 today. We hit an underground oil dump at Munich. It was more or less a milk run. We had a little Flak after bombs away. None of it hit us though and we got back O.K.

From the diary of S/Sgt Niel Jorgenson:

"13"th Mission

Target - Near Munich

Flak - Light inaccurate
Fighters - 2 groups 51's close support

Damage - None
Altitude - 25,500.

Troubles Encountered - Bomb bay doors inop. Flew over Swiss Alps.

Ships Name - "Out House Mouse"

"Mission Sheet" of S/Sgt George Odenwaller:

MISSION:	*#20*
TARGET:	*FREIHAM*
FLAK:	*MODERATE*
FIGHTERS:	*NONE*
DAMAGE:	*NONE*
TAKE-OFF:	*08:00*
LANDED:	*17:15*
T.T:	*9 HOURS - 15 MIN*
OXYGEN TIME:	*5 HOURS*
BOMB LOAD:	*5 1000 LB. BOMBS*
SHIP No:	*636*
NAME:	*OUTHOUSE MOUSE OR-N*
TEMP:	*- 30 F.*

From the diary of S/Sgt Walter Limberger:

#20
Target — Frieham, Ger.
Flak — Moderate
Fighters — None
Damage — None
Take Off — 0800 hrs
Landed — 1715 hrs
Total Time — 9 hrs 15 min
Oxygen — 5 hrs
Bombs — 5-1000 lb G. P.'s
Altitude — 25,500 ft.

Ship # — 636 Out House Mouse

Temp — -36°

Wasn't too bad today. Our missions are getting longer as our ground forces are getting deeper into Germany. Flew over the Alps again still deep in snow. Beautiful sight.

NEWSPAPER CLIPPING - (Source unknown)

No Milk Run Here

"WEE WILLIE" FROM OUR GROUP — 2 MEN CAME BACK AFTER V�)DAY!

U.S. Army Air Force Photo

The massive blows of Allied air armadas have broken the back of the Luftwaffe, but the skies over Germany are not all lined with velvet. Here an 8th Air Force Fortress, one wing shot off by an Me109, plunges earthward after attacking an airfield near Oranienburg on Tuesday's record day. The 8th lost 25 bombers and eight fighters out of a force of 1,300 bombers and 850 fighters.

The personal notation by Lt. Harvey reads:
"WEE WILLIE" FROM OUR GROUP - 2 MEN CAME BACK AFTER VE-DAY !"

[Note in the caption that this loss occurred in yesterdays battle near Oranienburg – grh]

[Page 185 of the book <u>The Ragged Irregulars of Bassingbourn</u> has a series of photographs of this loss. Its caption indicates that "Wee Willie", 231333, was on its 128th mission on April 8 and was the second to last B-17 lost in combat by the 91st Bomb Group. Page 240, of <u>Plane Names and Fancy Noses</u>, indicated there were no survivors from Lt. Robert Fullers nine man crew. However, Lt. Harvey's notation indicates differently.

Nine days later, the last B-17 lost in combat, "Skunkface III", 44-6568, Piloted by Lt. Harry Camp, was attacked by fighters while on its bomb run over the rail center at Dresden. She was last seen as she lost altitude and fell out of formation. Only the tail gunner, Herman Evans, survived from that crew of nine. <u>Plane Names and Fancy Noses</u>, page 201. – grh]

1,300 8th Heavies Again
Blast Reich as Nazis Hide

The air paths of 8th Air Force bombers and fighters were clear of enemy fighters yesterday after Tuesday's destructive raids on jet fighter bases, and over 1,300 heavies and more than 850 fighters carried the 8th's non-stop offensive into its ninth day by striking at airfields, rail targets, ordnance stores and oil objectives in southern Germany.

Two airfields, five marshalling yards, two oil storage depots, two ordnance depots and an explosives factory were hit. All targets were located in the areas of Munich, Nuremberg and Regensburg.

RAF bombers attacked in the same area when Halifaxes unloaded over railway yards at Nuremburg and at Bayreuth, north of Nuremberg. RAF also reported that its attacks on Kiel Monday night resulted in the sinking of the German pocket battleship Scheer.

Latest tabulations of damage wrought by 8th fighters Tuesday show that eight new records were hung up by the Thunderbolts and Mustangs, including the total bag of 305 planes and the 339th Mustang Group's destruction of 100 ships on the ground.

The 56th Thunderbolt Group, leading fighter outfit, became the first group to reach the 900 mark in destruction when it KO'd two in the air and 39 on the ground to boost its total to 904, of which 684 were killed in the air. One squadron of the 339th made a new squadron mark by knocking off 62, and the day's total of 284 blasted on the ground by all groups st a new mark for the 8th in strafing.

Lt. Col. John D. Landers, of Joshua, Tex., established a new individual record in ground kills by getting eight, and Lt. Col. Joseph L. Thury, of St. Paul, Minn., destroyed four to up his ground strafing total to 18-1/2 and lead all 8th fighters in this respect. The 20 jets shot down by the fighters in air combat also created a new record.

End of Clipping

===

APRIL 12
BREAKFAST AT 335, BRIEFING AT 435. OFF TO BAYREUTH, GERMANY.
MISSION SCRUBBED DUE TO WEATHER OVER U.K. AND CONTINENT.
SCRUBB #12.
GOT MORE TIME IN SACK - UNTIL 1100 A.M. TO BE EXACT. FLEW PRACTICE FORMATION
BUT HAD TO ABORT DUE TO GAS LEAK IN BOMBAY [sic].
WENT TO BIG "C" TO SEE THE PICTURE "WILSON".

From the diary of Lt. Phil Darby:

*A front has moved in over the Channel. We were to fly "Little Skunk Face" in the 401 Sqd. Mission
was scrubbed and the 8th was grounded [8th Air Force - grh]*

From the diary of Lt. Paul Katz:

Weather standown [sic] *today. No flying. Up on the list for tomorrows mission.*

===

APRIL 13
BREAKFAST AT 815, BRIEFING AT 915. OFF TO NEW MUNSTER[sic], GERMANY. BEAUTIFUL
WEATHER.
SAW NO FLAK OR FIGHTERS. ONE FORMATION DROPPED BOMBS ON ANOTHER AND TWO
SHIPS WERE LOST BY DIRECT HITS. ONE EXPLODED. THE OTHER LOST A WING AND SPUN
IN.
BOMBED RAILWAY CENTER WITH 10-500 LB. BOMBS. BOMBING RESULTS WERE
EXCELLENT. 8 HR. MISSION.

MISSION #23 COMPLETE.

OUR 48HR PASS BEGAN TONITE[sic] AT 1700 HRS. NATURALLY WE DID NOT LAND UNTIL
2000 HRS.

From the diary of Lt. Phil Darby:

Mission #15
Mission to New Munster.

From the diary of Lt. Paul Katz:

Number 22 today. We hit a marshalling yards at Neumunster in Denmark. It was our secondary target. The primary was overcast. It was a milk run more or less, got back O.K. going [sic] on pass.

From the diary of S/Sgt Niel Jorgenson:

=Friday= [the 13th] Fourteenth Mission

Target - Neumunster, Germany

Flak - Far off
Fighters - One grp 51's close support. 17 hit by bomb went down.

Damage - None
Altitude - 19,500 Ft.

Troubles Encountered - #4 R.P.M. gage out.

Ships Name - "Out House Mouse"

"Mission Sheet" of S/Sgt George Odenwaller:

MISSION:	*#21*
TARGET:	*NEUMUNSTER*
FLAK:	*NONE*
FIGHTERS:	*NONE*
DAMAGE:	*NONE*
TAKE-OFF:	*11:50*
LANDED:	*18:50*
T.T:	*7 HOURS*
OXYGEN TIME:	*4 HOURS*
BOMB LOAD:	*10 500 LB. BOMBS*
ALT:	*20,000 FT*
SHIP No:	*636*
NAME:	*OUTHOUSE MOUSE OR-N*
TEMP:	*- 24 F..*

GOOD MISSION - NO FLAK OR FIGHTERS FOR US: HOWEVER, DID SEE 2 B-17's GO DOWN - A/C WERE DROPPED ON BY ABOVE ELEMENT OVER TARGET: 1 B-17 BLEW UP - THE OTHER WENT DOWN IN A TIGHT LEFT SPIN - NO CHUTES FROM EITHER A/C. AWFUL TO WATCH !

From the diary of S/Sgt Walter Limberger:

#21

Target – Neumunster, Ger.

Flak – None

Fighters – None

Damage – None

Take Off – 1150 hrs

Landed – 1850 hrs

Total Time – 7 hrs

Oxygen – 5 hrs

Bombs – 10-500 lb G. P.'s

Ship # – 636 Out House Mouse

Altitude – 20,000 ft

Temp – -24°

Nice mission. No fighters or flak. Regardless, 2-B-17's went down. Bombers of high squadron dropped their bombs on them. One plane blew apart; other one went down in a tight spin. I saw no parachutes from either. Gut wrenching feeling also.

NEWSPAPER CLIPPING - (Source unknown)

8th Fighters
KO 261 Planes

Fighters of the 8th Air Force again tore into the Luftwaffe yesterday when over 350 Mustangs and Thunderbolts peeled off from escorting 200 bombers in an attack on railroad yards, 20 miles south of Kiel, to destroy 266 more planes parked on landing strips in this area.

Thus, for the second time in a week, the fighters eclipsed the record bag of 177 they set last September, and when the ace 56th Thunderbolt Group yesterday took a toll of 95 planes, the one-time group record was also surpassed for the second time in the week.

The destruction brought to 762 the total number of Nazi planes destroyed by the 8th since the fighters and bomber gunners knocked out 104 last Saturday. The Luftwaffe put up no opposition and flak was light to medium.

The bombers, which plastered the yards at Neumunster, between Kiel and Hamburg, had excellant weather over the targets.

End of Clipping

APRIL 14

FINALLY MADE IT OUT OF BED AT 8:00. CAUGHT THE 10:50 TRAIN TO LONDON. WENT TO Q.M. STORE AND SPENT £5 [5-POUNDS] FOR SHOES AND TROUSERS. WENT TO THE PALACE THEATHER[sic] IN PICCADILY TO SEE SID FIELD IN "STRIKE IT AGAIN". VERY GOOD EVEN THO[sic] WE HAD TO STAND. ALSO WENT TO SEE "PHILLIS DIXIE"! IN EVENING PHIL, KITTY AND I WENT TO THE NUT. HOUSE.[sic] A GOOD TIME WAS HAD BY ALL.

WE STAYED AT THE JULES CLUB (R.C.). WE AT[e] AT THE GROVERNER HOUSE.

[Co-Pilot Phil Darby, and Nav. Paul Katz (i.e. "Kitty") - grh]

From the diary of Lt. Phil Darby:

Katz, Harvey and I went to London this A.M. We got a room at the Red Cross. Saw "Strike It Again" with Sid Field. After the show, we went to a private club, "The Nut House" and danced. Climbed into the sack at 0500 the next morning.

From the diary of Lt. Paul Katz:

48 hour pass.

[Entry dated April 14, 15, 1945 – grh]

APRIL 15

SLEPT LATE. IT WAS 1300 HRS WHEN WE FINALLY GOT UP. BOUGHT MATERIAL FOR BATTLE JACKET £1/14/6 [1-pound, 14 shillings, 6 pence - grh]. TOTAL SPENT ON CLOTHES THIS TRIP WAS £ 7 [7-lbs - grh]. WENT TO PICTURES IN P.M. "THE UNSEEN". QUITE GOOD. LEFT FOR ROYSTON AT 2105. A VERY ENJOYABLE 48HR. PASS WAS HAD EVEN THO[sic] WE WERE ROBBED OF 12 HOURS.

[The battle jacket was later known as the "Ike Jacket". Approved for Officers but not part of the official clothing issue - grh]

From the diary of Lt. Phil Darby:

We were so beaten down today - did a little shopping and saw a show down town. Had supper at the Grosvenor House and talked to a correspondent, just back from Germany, after eating.

APRIL 16
BREAKFAST AT 810, BRIEFING AT 910. OFF TO REGENSBURG, GERMANY.
MISSION QUITE GOOD. BOMBED A RAILROAD BRIDGE WITH 6-1000# BOMBS. OUR GROUP
WAS THE ONLY GROUPE TO HIT THE TARGET AND WE BLEW IT TO HELL ! FIGHTERS WERE
IN THE AREA. HEAVY FLAK JUST OVER THE TARGET. OUR SHIP WAS THE ONLY ONE NEAR
IT. WE GOT NO HITS BUT WE SURE TRIED TO GET ON THE OTHER SIDE OF THE FORMATION.
A MARSHALLING YARD SHORT OF THE TARGET WAS HIT (BY MISTAKE) AND HAD LOTS OF
BIG FIRES. LENGTH OF MISSION 8 HRS.

MISSION #24 COMPLETE.

From the diary of Lt. Phil Darby:

Mission #16
We went to Regensburg. Not much trouble, but it was a tiring day. I think we knocked the bridge out.

From the diary of Lt. Paul Katz:

Number 23 today. We hit a rail bridge at Regansburg. There was a bit of Flak but no fighters and we came off it alright. On list for tomorrow.

From the diary of S/Sgt Niel Jorgenson:

Fifthteenth Mission

Target - Regensburg, Germany

Flak - Moderate & accurate
Fighters - P-51's escourt

Damage - None

Altitude - 24,000 Ft.

Troubles Encountered - None

Ships Name - "Out House Mouse"

"Mission Sheet" of S/Sgt George Odenwaller:

```
MISSION:        #22
TARGET:         REGENSBURG
FLAK:           LIGHT
FIGHTERS:       IN AREA
DAMAGE:         SLIGHT
TAKE-OFF:       11:45
LANDED:         19:30
T.T.            7 HOURS - 45 MIN
OXYGEN TIME: 4 HOURS
BOMB LOAD:   6 1000 LB. G.P.'s
ALT:            24,000 FT
SHIP No:        636
NAME:           OUTHOUSE MOUSE  OR-N
TEMP:           - 36 F..
```

LIGHT FLAK OVER TARGET - NO ONE HIT - WE ALL MADE IT HOME !

From the diary of S/Sgt Walter Limberger:

#22

Target – Regensburg, Ger.

Flak – Light

Fighters – Same

Damage – None

Take Off – 1145 hrs

Landed – 1930 hrs

Total Time – 7 hrs 45 min

Oxygen – 4 hrs

Bombs – 6-1000 lb G. P.'s

Ship # – 636 Out House Mouse

Altitude – 20,000 ft

Temp – -36°

War is nearly over but still we keep bombing everywhere. Easy mission today. Flak over target, none of it hit us thankfully.

NEWSPAPER CLIPPING - (Source unknown)

8th, 15th AFs
Have Finished

Strategic Raps

In an Order of the Day commending all units under his USSTAF command, Gen. Carl Spaatz yesterday announced that the strategic air war of the 8th and 15th Air Forces is at an end and that from now on they must "operate with out tactical air forces in close co-operation with our armies.

"The strategic air war has been won with a decisiveness becoming increasingly evident as our armies overrun Germany," Spaatz declared.

The Order of the Day was released shortly after 1,200 8th Air Force Fortresses and Liberators returned from attacks on German marshalling yards in the Regensburg area of southern Germany and blows against defense positions in the Gironde area north of Bordeaux.

Approximately 750 heavies, with 850 Thunderbolts and Mustang escorts, crossed the western battle line for the first time since Friday to batter rail targets and communications at Regensburg and at the junctions of Landshut, Plattling and Straubing, to the south and east.

Fighter escorts peeled off to destroy 223 enemy planes at enemy airfields in the Munich area and as far east as Prague in Czechoslovakia.

Meanwhile, 450 unescorted Fortresses dumped high explosives near Point de Grave on the west side of the Gironde estuary in co-operation with elements of the French Army moving against the cornered Germans at Bordeaux.

RAF Mosquitoes raided Berlin three times Sunday night, reporting very little flak and no fighter opposition, although the Germans turned on the capitol's searchlights for the first time in ma[n]y weeks.

End of Clipping

===

APRIL 17
BREAKFAST AT 6:50, BRIEFING AT 750. OFF TO DRESDEN, GERMANY.
BOMBED MARSHALLING YARDS WITH 12-500# BOMBS. 12 GROUPES WENT IN ON YARDS.
FLAK MODERATE AND ACCURATE. POPPED UP EVERYWHERE. GOT A FEW FLAK HOLES.
FIGHTER (262's) HIT OUR SQD. NO SHIPS LOST BUT A LOT OF CASUILTIES[sic]. OUR
ELEMENT GOT THREE FIGHTERS ON OUR TAIL. ELEMENT LEADER GOT HIT BAD, BALL

TURRET DIRECT HIT AND GUNNER FELL OUT OF TURRET. HIS TAIL GUNNER ALSO HIT BAD
BUT ALIVE I THINK. MY UPPER LOCAL GUNNER LET GO A BURST OF 400 RDS. ALL MY
GUNNERS SHOT UP THE FIGHTER.
MISSION 9-1/2 HRS LONG.

MISSION #25 COMPLETE

THANK GOD WE ARE HOME !

[The limited personal comments in Lt. Harvey's diary emphasize the few he does make. This mission must
have been hell ! Some minor notes: Due to the small space, ball turret gunners could not wear their
parachute while in the turret making the scene potentially even more horrific to witness. "My upper local
gunner" would have been S/Sgt. Niel Jorgenson, the flight engineer. From his normal position between and
behind the pilot and co-pilot, the engineer could turn and stand to operate the top turret gun during aerial
combat. - grh]

From the diary of Lt. Phil Darby:

Mission #17
*Dresden - I'll never forget it. Me262's hit our element just after we left the target. A sight that will
live in my mind forever; that ball turret gunners limp body hanging from his safety belt and
swinging in the air. Finally it dropped, and he didn't have a chance (no chute). The tail gunner
also hit. The "Jet" that had us singled out broke away under the hail of fire from Jorgenson and
Limberger.* [flight engineer on the top turret and the tail gunner - grh] *Flak was heavy and
accurate. Our ship was "Anxious Angel". "Out House Mouse" is getting an engine change.*

[Per The Ragged Irregulars, pg. 223, "Anxious Angel' was assigned to the 401st – tail number 338035
- grh]

From the diary of Lt. Paul Katz:

Number 24 today. Our target was a marshaling [sic] yard at Dresden. I saw a boy die
today. It was the first (and I hope the last) time I actually saw anyone killed. We reached
our objective on time and then it happened. They through [sic] up everything they had at us.
Flak and Jet fighters. We got out of the Flak alright but these jets made a pass at our
element. J-Jig [apparently the name of the aircraft – grh] who was leading our element was hit. Two
37mm shells hit it. One in the tail and one in the ball turret. The one that hit the ball turret
smashed it open and got the gunner. He fell out but his leg got hung up and he lay there
dangling in the air dead for about three minutes. The vibrations and air finally shook him loose
and he fell the 21,000 feet [to] the ground. It was horrible. I will remember how he looked as
long as I can remember. We finally got back to the base without any casualties.

From the diary of S/Sgt Niel Jorgenson:

Sixteenth Mission

Target - Dresden, Germany

Flak - Heavy over target
Fighters - ME-262's made pass 07:30 high in a pursuit curve. Shot 400 rds [rounds]. One burst stopped him & two 51's jumped him.

Damage - None
Altitude - 21,000 Ft.

Troubles - None

Ships Name - "Anxious Angel" - 401st

"Mission Sheet" of S/Sgt George Odenwaller

MISSION:	*#23*
TARGET:	*DRESDEN*
FLAK:	*MODERATE*
FIGHTERS:	*ME-262's*
DAMAGE:	*NONE*
TAKE-OFF:	*09:45*
LANDED:	*19:30*
T.T:	*9 HOURS - 45 MIN*
OXYGEN TIME:	*4 HOURS*
BOMB LOAD:	*12 500 LB. G.P.'s*
ALT:	*21,000 FT*
SHIP No:	*636*
NAME:	*OUTHOUSE MOUSE OR-N*
TEMP:	*- 36 F..*

A BUSY ONE TODAY - SOME FLAK - VERY ACCURATE OVER TARGET: AFTER BOMBS AWAY & ON OUR 180 TURN LEFT, 3 ME-262's HIT OUR ELEMENT - THE LEAD A/C HAD IT'S BALL TURRET GUNNER BLOWN OUT OF HIS TURRET BY 30mm CANNON - THE TAIL GUNNER ALSO WAS GONE - THIS A/C WAS RIGHT NEXT TO US - I BELIEVE I GOT ONE OF THE 163's - AS HE WAS SMOKING AS HE WENT UNDER ME: I COULD SEE HIS FACE LOOK UP AT ME AS HE WENT BY UNDER ME - WAS HIT AGAIN BY THE ME 262's A MOMENTS LATER. THIS TME CHASED BY P-51's.
OUR LEAD B-17G WAS "BLOOD & GUTS", A/C No. 48324 OF THE 401st BOMB SQD, CODE LL-R
WE MADE IT BACK O.K. !

NOTE: THESE ME 262's ATTACKED US FROM 6 O'CLOCK LEVEL - VERY FAST A/C.

[S/Sgt. Odenwaller states that "the lead a/c...was right next to us" and gives the name of the aircraft as "Blood & Guts". In a conversation with Phil Darby, the co-pilot, he stated that the plane was on "his side" thus it would have been on the right side of the "Anxious Angel" making them the left wing-man of the lead a/c "Blood & Guts". With the close formations flown by the B-17's, they would have been little more than a wing-length away from "Blood & Guts" during this attack.   NOTE: In his book, Plane Names & Fancy Noses, Ray Bowden lists this aircraft name and tail number as "Blood 'n' Guts".

More information from George follows the diary entry of S/Sgt Limberger below. – grh]

From the diary of S/Sgt Walter Limberger:

#23
Target – Dresden, Ger.
Flak – Moderate
Fighters – ME 262's
Damage – None
Take Off – 0945 hrs
Landed – 1930 hrs
Total Time – 9 hrs 45 min
Oxygen – 4 hrs
Bombs – 12-500 lb G. P.'s
Ship # – 035 Anxious Angel
Temp – -30°

Thought we had it today. Plenty of flak, but didn't get hit – very accurate though. After bombs away, 3 jets jumped our 3 plane element. I fired without hitting the one on my tail section. My guns jammed several times still not able to score a hit on him. Top turret Neil Jorgenson was firing also as the 262 went down underneath us. The plane next to us was hit hard. Ball turret gunner was hit with 30 millimeter cannon fire and blasted completely out of the turret and tail gunner also wounded but still alive. Later, another lone fighter came on my tail. Still my guns wouldn't fire properly. Found out later after mission that brass on ammunition clips were corroded due to dampness in U.K. 2 P-51's came at the fighters. Don't know if they got him. I thank the Lord we got back without a scratch.

[George Odenwaller provided me a copy of a draft letter he wrote April 6, 1996 where he related some of his combat flying experiences. The following further describes this mission:

"I know I got one and possibly two ME-262's – both came around from the 6 o'clock level [behind – grh] together and at about 600 yard out. As I fired, the a/c on the left blew out black smoke and then at about 300 yards out the a/c on the right belched black smoke and fire in his port [left] engine. [He] flew right under me while looking up at me – I saw his face. As I wheeled the turret to the left to follow them, both broke left and dived away.

When I came back around right, I got a look at the a/c flying on our starboard [right] – it was "Blood 'N Guts" a/c No. 48324, LL-R of the 401st B.S. [bomb squadron]. The tail gunner's guns were pointing in 2 different directions, the rear window was blown in and no tail gunner to be seen.

Then I saw the ball turret: the 2-inch thick glass plate was apparently blown into the gunner who was then blown out the back of the turret – empty with the headset and heated suit electric cables trailing out the front of the ball – gunner gone.

We both were targets [but] Lindy and I didn't get hit." – grh]

NEWSPAPER CLIPPING - (Source unknown)

8th Fighters Add 200
To Bag of Nazi Planes

Fighters of the 8th Air Force continued to ram home the finishing punches to their apparently defenseless, beaten foe, the Luftwaffe, when more than 850 Thunderbolts and Mustangs, which covered approximately 1,000 Liberators and Fortresses on forays deep into southern Germany and Czechoslovakia yesterday, bagged another 200 grounded enemy aircraft. Thus, the two-day toll taken by the fighters climbed to 941 and set the number put out of action in the last nine days at 1,651. Since Continent-based fighters and bombers have accounted for hundreds more at the same time, the Luftwaffe has in this period received what looks like a mortal blow.

Associated Press reported yesterday from SHAEF that the Luftwaffe's strength had been estimated recently at 4,000 planes. Since Apr.8, then, Allied fighters had destroyed roughly half this number. And, as a USSTAF staff officer indicated yesterday, the blows against the German Air Force will go on daily at the same terrific tempo.

Accentuating the statement by Gen. Carl Spaatz, USSTAF Commander, that the strategic was is over and U.S. air operations will now be designed strictly for cooperation with ground forces, this official declared that every parked German plane is a potential threat to advance Allied columns and must be put out of the way. He said many of the planes destroyed in Monday's record kill of 741 were one- and two-engined fighters capable of raising hob once they get off the ground.

The bombers also marked the transition to all-out tactical warfare by ranging deep into the shrinking Nazi corridor at the southern end of the fronts to pound three railway centers in Dresden and five rail junctions and an underground oil storage depot in Czechoslovakia.

The junctions were at Kladno, Beraun, Karlsbad, Falkenau and Aussig, and the depot at Roudnice, all near Prague. Four jet-propelled Nazi fighters made a weak stab at one formation of heavies but were driven off immediately by the U.S. fighters.

End of Clipping

==

APRIL 18
BREAKFAST AT 6, BRIEFING AT 7:00. OFF TO ROSESHIEM, GERMANY.
DID "S" TURNS ALL THE WAY TO AND FROM TARGET. [Usually this is done to "slow down" a portion of a formation to allow stragglers to form-up. - grh]. FLEW FOR ABOUT 30 MINUTES OVER THE ALPS. A BEAUTIFUL SIGHT TO SEE ! BOMBED A MARSHALLING YARDS[sic] WITH 12-500# BOMBS. SAW NO FIGHTERS BUT EVERYONE ON THE CREW [W]AS QUITE NERVOUS AFTER YESTERDAY. FLAK WAS LITE[sic] BUT QUITE ACCURATE. ALL IN ALL A GOOD MISSION TODAY. MISSION TIME WAS 9-1/2 HRS.

MISSION #26 COMPLETE

From the diary of Lt. Phil Darby:

Mission #18
Mission to Rosensheim. Rather uneventful, with some flak. We caught heavy prop wash over the Alps. They were pretty with snow, but I didn't enjoy them.

From the diary of Lt. Paul Katz:

Stood down today.

From the diary of S/Sgt Niel Jorgenson:

Seventeenth Mission

Target - Rosenheim, Germany

Flak - Light, accurate
Fighters - 51's escourt

Damage - None

Altitude - 17,500 Ft.

Troubles - None

Ships Name - "Lady Freda" "324"

["324" refers to the 324th BS at Bassingbourn as indicated by the DF portion of the radio designation given by S/Sgt Odenwaller below. The book, The Ragged Irregulars of Bassingbourn, lists the full DF-P designation as belonging to "Sweet Freda"of the 324th Squadron. While the book indicates there was a B-17 named "Lady Freda", its tail number and radio designation are unknown. "Out House Mouse" may still be getting that engine change - grh]

MISSION: #24
TARGET: RESENHEIM
FLAK: LIGHT - ACCURATE
FIGHTERS: NONE
DAMAGE: NONE
TAKE-OFF: 09:30
LANDED: 18:30
T.T: 9 HOURS
OXYGEN TIME: 4 HOURS 30 MIN
BOMB LOAD: 12 500 LB. G.P.'s
ALT: 18,000 FT
SHIP No: 772
NAME: SWEET FREDA   DF-P
TEMP: - 12 F.

   GOOD MISSION - LONG BUT EASY. ACCURATE LIGHT FLAK !

From the diary of S/Sgt Walter Limberger:

#24

Target – Rosenheim, Ger.

Flak – Light

Fighters – None

Damage – None

Take Off – 0930 hrs

Landed – 1830 hrs

Total Time – 9 hrs

Oxygen – 4-1/2 hrs

Bombs – 12-500 lb G. P.'s

Ship # – 772 Sweet Freda

Altitude – 18,000 ft

Temp – -12

Nice mission compared to last one yesterday. It was long but easy an[d] fairly warm. Flak was fairly light but accurate. Only a few missions left. Pray to get finished safely.

NEWSPAPER CLIPPING - (Source unknown)

Heavies Bomb
Rail Targets

While fighters of the 8th Air Force had a lean day in continuing their drive on Nazi airfields - early reports last night showed only one plane destroyed on the ground - more than 750 Fortresses and Liberators again swung deep into western Czechoslovakia and southern Germany yesterday to bomb marshalling yards in seven localities ahead of the advancing 3rd Army.

Approximately 600 Thunderbolts and Mustangs went along to cover the heavies and blast fields in the same areas. Whether the Luftwaffe had withdrawn its planes from these fields or had lost what it had in the area was not disclosed. But some enemy craft did appear during the long mission and fighters shot down three.

The marshalling yards attacked, mostly in small localities, were near Prague, Pilsen, and Regensburg. Weather was generally clear.

Four bombers and one fighter are missing.

Nearly 1,000 RAF bombers, covered by Mustangs and Spitfires, bombed Heligoland in the afternoon and also struck an airfield on the island of Dune.

End of Clipping

===

APRIL 19
GROUPE STAND-DOWN. REGULAR MORNING MEETING. FLEW PRACTICE FORMATION MISSION IN A.M. COMMUNICATIONS LECTURE IN P.M. WENT TO A HERO'S MEETING (PRESENTATION OF AWARDS) IN THE EVENING. I GOT TWO CLUSTERS. EARLY TO BED AGAIN.

From the diary of Lt. Phil Darby:

A group stand down today. There had been very little doing.

From the diary of Lt. Paul Katz:

Stood down again today.

===

APRIL 20
UP AT 7:10 TO FLY A PRACTICE MICKY MISSION. ALTITUDE OF 18,000 FT. SPENT ALL A.M. IN AIR. WENT TO BIG "C" IN P.M. [Cambridge - grh] TO HAVE BATTLE JACKET MADE. (£6/6 COST) [6-pounds, 6-shillings - grh]. CAME HOME EARLY AND TO BED SOON. TO DAY[sic] HAS BEEN SQD, STAND-DOWN.

From the diary of Lt. Phil Darby:

Squadron stand down. I didn't go into town, but stayed on the base and wrote letters and slept.

From the diary of Lt. Paul Katz:

Went up for number 25 today. Target, a rail bridge at Munich. It wasn't to[sic] bad. We had a little Flak but no fighters. Got back O.K.

===

APRIL 21
BREAKFAST AT 3:15, BRIEFING AT 4:15. OFF TO MUNICH, GERMANY.
LOTS OF QUITE BAD WEATHER, CLIMBED 10,000 FT. THRU[sic] CIRRUS CLOUDS. SAW NO FIGHTERS. FLAK WAS LITE AND INACCURATE. BOMBED RAILWAY MARSHALLING YARDS PIFF [instrument bombing. See Lt. Darby below. - grh] WITH 6-500# G.P. PLUS 6-M17 INCINDERARY BOMBS. BUCKEYE BLUE (SCOUTING FORCE) WENT DOWN ON THE DECK [dropped to a very low altitude – grh] AFTER BOMB IMPACT TO SEE DAMAGE. THE REPORT "DON'T THINK YOU BOYS WILL EVER HAVE TO COME BACK TO MUNICH AGAIN. THE WHOLE DAMNED CITY IS ON FIRE." GOOD DEAL !
LENGTH OF MISSION 9-1/2 HOURS.

MISSION #27 COMPLETE.

GROUPE PARTY TONITE[sic] - THINK I SHALL SLEEP INSTEAD.

From the diary of Lt. Phil Darby:

Mission #19
It was a very cloudy day and we were forced to bomb the center of Munich on instruments. Our original target was a Jet air field. I saw one burst of flak, but I understand there was much more. Very long & tiring mission.

From the diary of Lt. Paul Katz:

Number 26 today. We bombed Munich again. P.F.F. this time [bombing by radar. See entries below – grh]. *The weather was pretty bad and we had a pretty hard time getting thru* [sic] *a front. O.K. otherwise.*

From the diary of S/Sgt Niel Jorgenson:

Eighteenth Mission

Target - Munich, Germany

Flak - Moderate inaccurate
Fighters - 51's escourt

Damage - None

Altitude - 25,000 Ft.   -36 C

Troubles - None

Ships Name - "Lewd Angel"

"Mission Sheet" of S/Sgt George Odenwaller:

MISSION:	#25
TARGET:	MUNICH
FLAK:	MODERATE
FIGHTERS:	NONE
DAMAGE:	NONE
TAKE-OFF:	06:00
LANDED:	15:00
T.T:	9 HOURS
OXYGEN TIME:	4 HOURS
BOMB LOAD:	6 500 LB. G.P.'s - 6 M-17 CLUSTERS & LEAFLETS
ALT:	25,000 FT
SHIP No:	755
NAME:	LEWD ANGLE LG-A
TEMP:	- 40 F.

VERY CLOUDY MISSION: HIT TARGET THRU 10/10 CLOUD COVER - BOMBED BY "MICKEY".

[10/10 clouds is zero visibility thus bombed by "Mickey". Mickey was radar. "Out House Mouse" is apparently still getting that engine change. – grh]

From the diary of S/Sgt Walter Limberger:

#25

Target – Munich, Ger.

Flak – Moderate

Fighters – None

Damage – None

Take Off – 0600 hrs

Landed – 1500 hrs

Total Time – 9 hrs

Oxygen – 4 hrs

Bombs – 6-500 lb G. P.'s 6-Incendiary Clusters

Altitude – 25,000 ft

Ship # – 014 Lewd Angel

Temp – -40°

Today's mission was a fairly easy one; quite long again. Visibility was poor but we bombed through 10/10's cloud cover hitting our target. Don't think we'll be on many more missions.

NEWSPAPER CLIPPING - (Source unknown)

8th Inactive After Striking Munich

Encountering adverse weather but no enemy planes, approximately 350 8th Air Force Fortresses, accompanied by about 400 Mustangs and Thunderbolts, Saturday bombed rail yards at Munich and Ingolstadt and an air field at Landsberg, 30 miles west of Munich, while Kiel was attacked by RAF Mosquitoes Saturday night.

Bombing was done through solid cloud except at Landsberg, where some bombardiers glimpsed the target. Six bombers are missing, but all fighters returned safely.

There were no operations reported by the 8th yesterday.

End of Clipping

==

APRIL 22
SLEPT UNTIL 11:30 TODAY. NICE FOR A CHANGE. THIS HAS BEEN A FULL DAY OF REST FOR ALL. SPENT THE DAY WRITING LETTERS AND READ. EARLY TO BED AGAIN.

From the diary of Lt. Phil Darby:

Stand down.

From the diary of Lt. Paul Katz:

8th Air Force Standowns [sic].
I think we've had it as far as being operational any more [sic].

[Entry dated April 22, 23, 24 – grh]
===

APRIL 23
REGULAR MORNING MEETING. GROUPE STAND-DOWN AGAIN. FLEW PRACTICE FORMATION MISSION IN P.M. PLAYED BRIDGE AND READ REMAINDER OF DAY. EARLY TO BED SO THAT I'LL GROW UP TO [be] BIG AND STRONG.

From the diary of Lt. Phil Darby:

Stand down.

===

APRIL 24
GROUP STAND-DOWN AGAIN. RUMOR HAS IT THAT THE 8TH AIR FORCE IS NO LONGER OPERATIONAL. IF WE DO NOT FLY ON THE MORROW IT WILL BE ALMOST PROOF. REGULAR MORNING MEETING.

FLEW SCS-51 (RUNWAY LOCALIZER) [As mentioned earlier, this is a form of radar approach - grh] GLIDE PATH WAS OUT SO WE FLEW A SHORT X-C [cross country - grh] WITH CO PILOT [sic] AS NAVIGATOR WITH BOMBARDIER AND ENGINEER THE PILOT - I ACTED AS CO-PILOT.

[Per conversations with surviving crew members, this was something Lt. Harvey did on his own from very early on. He wanted everyone on his crew to be able to bring the aircraft home and land it should it became necessary. For example, while George Odenwaller had washed out of flight training, the training he had completed might save the aircraft and its crew. – grh]

BRIDGE AND LETTERS IN EVENING.

TO BED EARLY AS USUAL.

From the diary of Lt. Phil Darby:

Stand down.

===

APRIL 25
BREAKFAST AT 2:00, BRIEFING AT 3:00. OFF TOO [sic] PILZEN (PILSEN)
CHECHOSLOVAKIA[sic].
WE BOMBED AIR FIELD, (JET) WITH 6-500 LBS PLUS 4 M17 INCENDERIES. ONLY SQD IN THE
GROUPE THAT HIT TARGET. OVER TARGET AND IN FLAK FOR 35 MINUTES DUE TO 360
DEGREE TURNS FOR SECOND RUN ON TARGET. FLAK WAS MODERATE BUT DAMNED
ACCURATE. OUR BOMBS HUNG UP AND WOULD NOT SALVO. LOST #3 ENGINE COMING OFF
TARGET. CONTROLL[sic] CABLES SHOT OUT (ELEVATOR & RUDDER) FLEW HOME ALONE.
LANDED AT HOME FIELD WITH NO MISHAP.
MISSION TIME 9-1/2 HRS.

ENGLISH RADIO ANNOUNCED OUR TARGET AT 9:00 AND TOLD PEOPLE THERE TO STAY
AWAY UNTIL AFTER 11:00. NO WONDER THERE WAS SO MUCH AND SUCH ACCURATE FLAK.

MISSION #28 COMPLETE.

[Additional comments follow the newspaper clipping - grh]

From the diary of Lt. Phil Darby:

Mission #20
*We bombed Pilzen, home of the Skoda Works. They threw up everything in the town. We made two
runs before bombs away. Then things began to happen. We lost No. 3 eng[ine] and a flak hit
severed three control cables. The engineer [S/Sgt Jorgenson] did a beautiful job of fixing them up
using nothing but wire and bare hands. We left formation. Eight P51's escorted us most of the way
out of Germany.*
(<u>Final Mission</u> - 91st B.G.)

[That must be a postscript as no one knows this fact yet. Peace is not announced to the G.I.'s until May 7,
1945 – grh]

From the diary of Lt. Paul Katz:

*Number 27 today. We hit an airfield at Pilzen. It was pretty rough. The Flak was right in
there and we had to make a few 360's over the target. Our controls were shot away and #3
engine went out so we had to leave the formation and go home alone. It wasn't too bad this time*

as I have a lot more experience than I had the last time it happened. We got back O.K.
although we never knew when the controls would go completely.

[This is the last diary entry for Lt. Katz – grh]

From the diary of S/Sgt Niel Jorgenson:

Nineteenth Mission

Target - Pilsen, Czechoslovakia

Flak - Moderate & accurate
Fighters - 51's close support

Damage - Control cables hit

Altitude - 22,000 Ft.

Troubles - Feathered #3 engine. Repaired two elevator & one rudder control cables. Cranked tail wheel up - bomb bay doors & salvo inoperative.

Ships Name - "Out House Mouse"

[When recalling this mission, Phil Darby said, "Jorgy went forward and cut a piece of wire out of something and returned and repaired 3 of the 5 damaged cables". Knowing each of the cables had very high tension, he is still amazed and does not know how S/Sgt Jorgenson managed to make his emergency repairs. From Czechoslovakia, the most direct return trip home crosses all of Germany. – grh]

"Mission Sheet" of S/Sgt George Odenwaller:

MISSION:	*#26*
TARGET:	*PILSEN (CHEC.)*
FLAK:	*HEAVY & ACCURATE*
FIGHTERS:	*NONE*
DAMAGE:	*MAJOR*
TAKE-OFF:	*05:45*
LANDED:	*15:00*
T.T:	*9 HOURS - 15 MIN*
OXYGEN TIME:	*5 HOURS*
BOMB LOAD:	*6 500 LB. G.P.'s & 6 M-17 CLUSTERS*
ALT:	*22,500 FT*
SHIP No:	*636*
NAME:	*OUTHOUSE MOUSE OR-N*
TEMP:	*- 36 F..*

A ROUGH ONE TODAY - HEAVY FLAK - MISSED TARGET - MADE A 360 LEFT & MADE THE RUN AGAIN THRU THE FLAK - 3 B-17's WENT DOWN NEARBY - ONE A DIRECT BOMB BAY HIT & EXPOLSION - THE OTHER 2 ROLLED OVER IN FLAMES - SAW ONLY 5 CHUTES FROM THOSE A/C.
OUR #3 ENGIN[sic] WAS KNOCKED OUT DURING BOMB RUN THEN OUR ELEVATOR CABLES WERE CUT BY FLAK - ONLY 2 OF 7 HELD - 'OL JORGENSON (ENGINEER) SPLICED BOTH CABLES TOGETHER & SAVED OUR ASSES - LINDY STAYED IN TAIL POSITION TO OPERATE RUDDER YOKE

BY HAND UPON LANDING - NO EASY TASK !   LEARNED LATER AT G-2 THAT 6 B-17's WENT DOWN ON THAT 2nd BOMB RUN.
                              VERY TIRED !!

["Lindy" would be Walter Limberger, the tail gunner. "G-2" is the Intelligence debriefing - grh]

From the diary of S/Sgt Walter Limberger:

#26
Target — Pilsen, Checz.
Flak — Heavy + Accurate
Fighters — None
Damage — Major
Take Off — 0545 hrs
Landed — 1500 hrs
Total Time — 9 hrs 15 min
Bombs — 6-500 lb G. P.'s 6-M17 Clusters
Altitude — 22,500 ft
Ship # — 636 Out House Mouse
Temp — -36°

Very rough mission. We got over target and flak was very heavy and accurate. We didn't drop our bombs, so we made a 360° turn and came over target again through all that flak. Going over and from target, I saw a direct hit on group behind us. The hit took out 3 planes with a single burst. I saw only 2 parachutes and both were on fire. Very sad to see.

Our #3 engine was knocked out — a direct flak hit did the damage. It also severed our elevator cables only 2 of 7 strands holding. Trim tabs also were damaged with 3 strands holding C. 1. also damaged.

Joe Pilot alerted us to be ready for bail out if any cable snapped. The Lord was with us as we got back to base safely. Joe Harvey (Pilot) asked me to land in tail as I could actuate cables from the yoke in my position which I did and he set it down like a feather Thank God. Note, I later learned there were 6 B-17's that were taken out of that direct hit as three must have been completely blown apart. (8 th Air Force Intellegence).

NEWSPAPER CLIPPING - (Source unknown)

Allies Bomb Berchtesgaden

Hitler's Bavarian redoubt trembled under Allied bombs yesterday as both 8th Air Force and RAF heavy bombers roared deep into southern Germany to blast Berchtesgaden and areas within 25 miles north of the Fuehrer's mountain lair.

Some 250 Liberators of a force of approxiamtely 550 U.S. bombers laid high explosives on railway targets in four localities near the mountain hideout, while two separate forces of RAF Lancasters, some carrying six-ton bombs, attacked Hitler's refuge and SS barracks in the town itself. The Lancasters, of which two are missing, were escorted by Mustangs of the 8th and of RAF Fighter Command.

Meanwhile, more that 300 Fortresses of the 8th bombed the Skoda armament works and an airfield in Pilsen, Czechoslovakia, in what was described as the first Allied raid made after a specific forewarning from SHAEF. Before the bombers hit their targets SHAEF broadcast to slave workers in the Skoda plant to "get out and stay out," for bombers were on their way to blast the factories.

U.S. airmen reported hot barrages of flak but no enemy air opposition, although one Nazi jet plane was shot down in combat by part of the force of over 500 Mustangs which provided cover for both missions. Sixteen bombers and three fighters failed to return.

Heavies of the 15th Air Force pounded the main station and railway yards at Linz, the most important communications center left in Austria, while Italy-based Thunderbolts ranged over northern Italy to bomb and strafe enemy supply columns ahead of the advancing 5th and 8th Armies.

Medium bombers and fighter-bombers of the 2nd TAF also hit in support of ground forces, hammering fortified positions inside Bremen.

End of Clipping

[The Pilsen raid was the last combat mission of the 8th Air Force and is detailed in the story: "The Last Mission of the 91st - Pandemonium Over Pilsen: The Forgotten Final Mission", by Lowell L. Getz, copyright 1997. The story may be read on the website of the 91st Bomb Group at:
http:/www.91stbombgroup.com/lastmission.html.

Several facts should be emphasized about this mission: (1) The newspaper article tells of the radio broadcast made while the bombers were in route to their target. (2) The crews had been instructed to only bomb after visually sighting the target. (3) The Germans had radios too, so the broadcast warning served to alert them as to the when and where of the attack and their anti-aircraft batteries were ready and waiting. With the accurate and intense flak and the order to only bomb on a visual, the bombers were nearly sitting ducks.

In the article, Mr. Getz tells of a vast amount of confusion on the bomb run when the lead bomb groups failed to visually locate their targets due to the heavy clouds and had therefore called for a 360 to make a second run on the target. However, others had found their targets and dropped their bombs and due to the heavy flak over the bomb run did not see a reason for making a 360 when they had no bombs. Instead of making the 360, some of these aircraft were making only a 180 and trying to form-up for the return to England.

The 91st Bomb Group was the last of the bomber stream and was flying into all of this confusion - some of the preceding aircraft making 360's and some not; the heavy flak with ever improving accuracy due to the second bomb run; and the conflicting orders coming over the radio. The participation of the "Out House Mouse" and its damage on this mission is specifically mentioned in Mr. Getz's story. In it he states that "She stayed in formation with the squadron on the first run. On the bomb run the "Outhouse Mouse" took a flak hit that knocked out the No. 3 engine and severed all but two of the elevator control cables. However, she was able to remain in formation as the 323rd made the 360 and went over the target again. After coming off the target the second time, "Outhouse Mouse" could not maintain her position and had to drop out of the formation to return alone on a more direct flight back to England."

There is a conflict between the Getz version and the diary entry of Lt. Harvey and his crew. Mr. Getz states that before her first bomb run, the "Outhouse Mouse" had already released her bomb load, while Lt. Harvey states that the bombs "...hung up and would not salvo." Mr. Odenwaller's mission sheet simply says that they "...missed target - made a 360 left & made the run again thru the flak". Lt. Harvey's version is further verified in his diary entry of the following morning when he states, "...had a big session with all the big wheels about our bombs hanging up on yesterdays mission." These two diary accounts clearly indicate to me that the "Out House Mouse" still had a bomb load when she made her second run because of the failure to salvo on the first run. Since no further mention is made about where the bombs were released, I feel it fair to assume that they were released over Pilsen. This has been confirmed in my conversations with surviving crew members. Some have even stated that S/Sgt Jorgenson "kicked the bombs out" on the second run. Whatever action there may have been, it was accomplished in a bomb bay whose doors remained open and inoperative and in an aircraft that is being tossed and blown around the sky by the concussions from the accurate flak bursts and limited control of the rear control surfaces. In a telephone conversation with Mr. Getz, he stated that due to the heavy and accurate flak, some crewmen he interviewed in his research were certain that they had made THREE bomb runs that day mistaking the returning 180 for the second of three bomb runs.

As noted in these diaries, the aircraft damage mentioned by Mr. Getz was accurate: the number 3 engine was out and five of seven rudder and elevator control cables were severed. Also stated in the diaries, the engineer, S/Sgt Jorgenson, spliced and/or tied some of the damaged cables together "using nothing but wire and bare hands". Phil Darby told me in a telephone conversation that those cables are under so much tension that to this day he doesn't know how S/Sgt Jorgenson managed to splice them together. With continued control of the aircraft in question, Walter Limberger's diary states that Lt. Harvey instructed his crew to be ready for the command to bail-out if he lost any of the few remaining cables as he struggled to get his badly wounded aircraft back to England. Any loss would have certainly placed the aircraft in an uncontrolled dive. Lindy also noted that, Lt. Harvey ask him to go into his tail gunner's position and manually work the rudder yoke during the landing. This was a clear violation of normal landing procedures and something Lt. Harvey was not known to do. These measures allowed the crew to return and land at their home base "...WITH NO MISHAP." - a typical understatement by Lt. Harvey. The final combat mission of the "Out House Mouse" and the 8th Air Force is complete – although they do not know that yet.

The Pilsen raid was the 139th combat mission of the "Out House Mouse" without an abort. Within the entire 8th Air Force, her combat record is surpassed only by that of her sister-ship, the "Nine-O-Nine", which is making its 140th combat mission. Both of these records stand as remarkable achievements of all of her aircrews and especially that of her ground support crew lead by M/Sgt. Rollin L. Davis.

Mr. Getz's research has revealed that the 323rd had 12 aircraft on this mission flying as the High Squadron in B-Group. The aircraft are in the following formation (names are from <u>Plane Names & Fancy Noses</u>):
    LEAD is Thompson in #7630 (OR-T) "Geraldine" with PFF capability. His left-wing is Hunt in #2116 (OR-B) "Hi-Ho Silver". His right-wing is Dean in #9225 (OR-V) No name or name unknown.

    On Thompson's left flying Low is Dickson in #7276 (OR-S) "Sweet 17". His left-wing is Harvey in #1636 (OR-N) "Out House Mouse". His right-wing is Martinson in #8379 (OR-O) "Margie". On Thompson's right flying High is Ward in #6615 (OR-M) Unknown. His left-wing is Schille in #6964 (LG-Y a 322nd aircraft) Unknown. His right-wing is Borgstrom in #7540 (OR-Z) Unknown.

    Behind Thompson is Blanchet in #1909 (OR-R) "Nine-O-Nine". His left-wing is Phagan in #8841 (OR-L) "Judy's Little Ass". His right-wing is Templeton in #3263 (OR-J) "Ragan's Raiders"

The reader may recall that Lt. Harvey mentions Lts. Thompson and Borgstrom on January 20 when they received their squadron assignments.

Notice that Lt. Harvey is flying "Low". In addition to all of the confusion concerning 360 turns etc., Phil Darby said that as they lined up for their bomb run, an aircraft was above them, with his bomb bay doors open and he kept drifting over the "Out House Mouse". They could look right up into that airplane and count their bombs. They were scared stiff that it would release its bombs and drop them right on top of them which would cut the Mouse to pieces. There was very little they could do, but pray because they were on their run with other B-17's following along behind them also setting up for their bombing runs. I can still hear Phil as he told me fifty years later, "It was really quite scary".

George Odenwaller, Lt. Harvey's ball turret gunner, tells the story of Lt. Harvey and some members of his crew walking around the "Out House Mouse" after they had been assigned to the ship, and of their disappointment in having been assigned an old beat-up aircraft while other crews were being assigned nice shiny new B-17's. As he put it, both the "Out House Mouse" and the "Nine-O-Nine" were "old and near to being war weary. Both were tired and had been patched, patched and patched again." One of the men who had been in the ETO for some time told them that they were <u>lucky</u> to be assigned that ship - for the "Out House Mouse" would take more damage than the newer aircraft and would bring them home when other ships would not.

George also tells of Lt. Harvey telling his crew that he was not going to bail out of a B-17 while it was moving forward. The attitude of Lt. Harvey and the support of his crew who never gave up on their ship; and the assignment of a war-torn and scarred but rugged aircraft that would not go down despite the extent of her damage, may have provided the "edge" that allowed my father and his crew to survive the war.

While I have personally thanked each of these men for helping bring my father home from the war; to a man all have refused to accept my thanks saying – and this is nearly a direct quote from each man – "No! Your father brought us home!"

I thank God that my father was in such good care during his time in the European Theater of Operations for this has allowed me to know 9 very brave men. – grh]

==

APRIL 26
HAD A BIG SESSION[sic] WITH ALL THE BIG WHEELS ABOUT OUR BOMBS HANGING UP ON YESTERDAYS MISSION. IT SEEMS ALL IS WELL NOW. THE[y] SEEMED TO THINK WE DROPPED ON OUR LINES BUT WE <u>KNOW</u> WE DID NOT.

WENT TO BIG "C" IN EVENING.

HAD CREWS PICTURE TAKEN IN FRONT OF "OUT HOUSE MOUSE"

[This crew picture appears at the beginning of the book. If one looks carefully, they will notice that a step ladder is in front of the #3 engine (inboard engine on the right side of the aircraft) and that the engine itself is missing. Repair of the damage on the Pilsen mission is already in progress. An unofficial crew photograph is also included in the photo section later in this book. That photograph was taken by the waist gunner, S/Sgt Allen Kus just after they had landed and before the crew had removed any of their flight equipment. Since Al could not recall the mission and no one mentioned it in their diary, the date of that crew photograph remains unknown but all agree that it does pre-date the official photograph. George Odenwaller thinks that it may have been taken April 10 after the Oranienburg mission. - grh]

From the diary of Lt. Phil Darby:

It is beginning to look like we have flown our last mission. The "Southern Redoubt" is the only area showing resistance in Germany. I am cursing the day I went into the hospital because I don't have the number of missions required for a tour (25).

[Shortly after the 8th Air Force began combat missions from England, the number of combat missions was set at 25 where the survival rate was estimated at 1 in 5. Later, as the war progressed, that number was raised to 30 and then to 35 when the 100 plane raids began. That is why Lt. Harvey stated it was "down hill" for him when on March 31 he completed his 18th mission. Now however, it seems that the original mission count is again important. – grh]

===

APRIL 27
REGULAR MORNING MEETING. AIR CRAFT REC [sic] IN P.M. PICTURES IN P.M. ALSO.
EARLY TO BED AGAIN.

From the diary of Lt. Phil Darby:

Rumors are beginning to circulate concerning the wars end and it is also rumored we are not operational (the 8th A.F.)

===

APRIL 28
MORNING MEETING. FLEW BLUE BOMB MISSION IN A.M. BUT DUE TO CLOUDS GOT ONLY ONE BOMB AWAY. LANDED EARLY.
WENT TO BIG "C" IN EVENING.

From the diary of Lt. Phil Darby:

3rd Division planes are dropping food to the Dutch. Still nothing doing.

===

APRIL 29
NO MEETING TODAY SINCE IT IS SUNDAY. SLEPT UNTIL NOON. SPENT DAY PLAYING
BRIDGE. PICTURES IN EVENING.

MANY RUMORS GOING AROUND THE BASE THESE DAYS AS TO WHERE, WHEN (AND WHO)
THE GROUPE IS LEAVING.

From the diary of Lt. Phil Darby:

*Just seem to be sweating out time. We had a crew picture taken today in front of "Out House
Mouse"*

Tonight we disposed of four bottles of Scotch. Sang songs and in general tore up the barracks.

===

APRIL 30
PAY DAY AGAIN.
LOTS OF RUMORS HERE. BIGGEST AND MOST OFFICIAL ONE IS THAT THE 91ST IS NO
LONGER OPERATIONAL. WE TURN IN OUR ESCAPE KITS TUESDAY AND THAT IS <u>NO</u> RUMOR.

WAS CHECKED OUT ON SCS-51 TO DAY [sic] BY CAPT. WARD.

WOULD YOU BELIEVE IT? IT WAS SNOWING TODAY. IN FACT ABOUT 3 INCHES OF SNOW IS
ON THE GROUND NOW.

BIG EVENT THIS MONTH WAS THE BIRTH OF A SON, GEORGE ROBERT, ON 2 APRIL AT
5:30A.M.

===

MAY 1
REGULAR MORNING MEETING. NO FLYING FOR PAST 3 OR 4 WEEKS. 48 HR PASS BEGAN AT
1700 HRS BUT LEFT FOR LONDON AT 1200. LITES[sic] STILL NOT ON IN LONDON. UNABLE TO
GET ROOMS AT JULES RED CROSS CLUB SO STAYED AT THE U.S. HOTEL. BOY WHAT A DIVE!

From the diary of Lt. Phil Darby:

*Our pass started today. Katz, Harvey and I went to London. We were unable to get a good room -
so finally settled for a cheap hotel, the "U.S. Hotel". A Limy negro woman ran the place.*

===

MAY 2
SLEPT LATE AND STILL IN LONDON. FINALLY GOT A ROOM IN JULES CLUB.
TODAY THE QUEEN OF ENGLAND, (ELIZABETH) AND DAUGHTER (PRINCESS ELIZABETH)
VISITED THE JULES CLUB AT 1600 HRS. THE QUEEN AND PRINCESS SPOKE TO PAUL, PHIL
AND I. WE HAD OUR PICTURES TAKEN WHILE SPEAKING TO THEM. THEY ARE QUITE NICE
AND MUCH, MUCH BETTER IN APPEARANCE AND MANNER THAN PICTURES MAKE THEM
SEEM.

From the diary of Lt. Phil Darby:

*A hard night. we secured rooms early at the Jules Club. In the P.M. Queen Elizabeth and the
Princess visited the Club. We had our pictures taken with them.*

[The then Princess is the current Queen Elizabeth II seen at the extreme right of the photograph. – grh]

The caption reads: Her Majesty at the American Red Cross Jules Club for Officers talking with, left to right,
Lieutenants Paul Katz of Brooklyn: Elmer Harvey, of Boone, Iowa, and Ben Heyden, of St. Louis.

[Notice that Lt. Paul Katz is wearing his glasses. Photograph provided by Mrs. Joan Katz. – grh]
===

MAY 3

ANOTHER DAY BUT NO EXCITEMENT. WENT TO CHECK ON BATTLE JACKET BUT ALL
SHOPES[sic] CLOSED TO DAY.
BED EARLY. AGAIN.
PASS OF 48HRS IS ABOUT OVER FOR ANOTHER TWO WEEKS.

From the diary of Lt. Phil Darby:

*Spent the day strolling about London and talking to friends I bumped into at the Red Cross. Had a
lengthy conversation with a jeweler. He invited me to dinner.*

==

MAY 4

MORNING MEETING AS USUAL. FLEW A MICKEY MISSION BUT DUE TO LOW CEILINGS (1000
FT) MADE A X-C [cross country flight - grh] OVER SOUTHERN ENGLAND. VERY INTERESTING
AND BEAUTIFUL. SAW THE COASTAL TOWN WHERE INVASION WAS EXPECTED ALSO.
EARLY TO BED. AGAIN.

From the diary of Lt. Phil Darby:

Cooper and yours truly got a little oiled in the bay. It was a going away party for Bob Hodgkins.

==

MAY 5

REGULAR MEETING TODAY. NO FLYING SINCE THE SQD OFFICER PLAYED THE E.M. [enlisted
men - grh] SOFTBALL. OFFICERS LOST !
WERE TOLD TODAY BY C.O. THAT ALL WITH OVER 25 MISSIONS THEIR TOUR WOULD NO
DOUBT BE COMPLETE. HAD TWO SHOTS IN ARM AND CAN HARDLY MOVE. GROUND
SCHOOL IN P.M.
MADE A TRIP INTO BIG "C" IN EVENING AND IT RAINED LIKE HELL ALL THE TIME SO ALL I
MANAGED TO GET DONE WAS GET SOAKED !

From the diary of Lt. Phil Darby:

Peace rumors are very strong now. Marty, Joe and I went on a practice bombing mission.

==

MAY 6

AGAIN TODAY I GOT TO SLEEP QUITE LATE. IN FACT I JUST ABOUT MISSED DINNER !

WENT TO PICTURES IN P.M. "DRAGON SEED".

EARLY TO BED. ABOUT 2 A.M. LT. PITTS WAS TIGHT AND KEPT THE WHOLE BAY UP. HE IS BETTER THAN A SHOW !

From the diary of Lt. Phil Darby:

Another slow day. Raber and I went into Royston tonight. Had a few beers and came home.

==

MAY 7

REGULAR MORNING MEETING. RATHER QUIET DAY. ABOUT 11:10HRS TANHOY (P.A. SYSTEM) ANNOUNCED THAT ALL PERSONNEL THIS STATION TO MEET A[t] PARADE GROUND A[t] 1200 HRS. ALL THE GROUPE RESTRICTED AS OF 1110 HRS.

THE NOON MEETING ANNOUNCED THAT THE ARMISTACE HAD BEEN SIGNED ABOUT 11:30 LAST NITE[sic]. WAR IS OVER IN EUROPE BUT AS YET NO ONE KNOWS IT EXCEPT THE ARMED FORCES.

THANK GOD THAT AT LEAST THIS MUCH DEATH AND SADNESS HAS BEEN BROUGHT TO A HALT.

[Another personal understatement of Lt. Harvey - grh]

From the diary of Lt. Phil Darby:

Col. Terry [Commander at Bassingbourn -grh] *called us all together and announced the war had ended, but wasn't to be announced until tomorrow. A big drinking bout took place on the base as everyone is restricted. Coop and I made it an evening of beer at the Club.*

==

MAY 8

BIG PARTY ALL OVER THE BASE. TWO-DAY HOLIDAY DECLARED.
ALL U.S. ARMY RESTRICTED TO BASES UNTIL 0700 A.M. TOMORROW. [Note: At this time this is the Army Air Corp not the Air Force - grh]. OFFICIAL ANNOUNCEMENT OF WARS END MADE HERE A[t] 1500 HRS BY PRES. TRUEMAN[sic]. (TIME IN U.S. WAS 0900 A.M.)
MANY RUMORS HERE BUT NOTHING OFFICAL[sic].

From the diary of Lt. Phil Darby:

This is it! V-E Day. We are not permitted in town. The British are sure whooping it up. So are we. Setting off flares with very pistols [sic], *everyone is tight.*

[A very pistol is a flare gun. When returning from a mission, they would fire a red flare if they had wounded on board. No doubt all in England are cheering the end of a war that began for them in 1939. They have endured more years of war than any of the other allies. – grh]

151

==

MAY 9
RESTRICTION LIFTED TODAY. THIS ALSO IS A HOLLIDAY[sic].
WENT TO BIG "C" TO SEE HOW THE NATIVES TOOK THE WARS END. MOST ALL WERE GAY
THO[sic] ONLY TWO PUBS WERE OPEN SINCE THE ARMED FORCES WERE IN TOWN.

CAME HOME EARLY. QUITE BORING DAY SPENT IN TOWN.

From the diary of Lt. Phil Darby:

We are given [t]his day off with the exception of an insignificant ground school schedule.

==

MAY 10
BACK TO WORK TODAY.
BREAKFAST AT 6:00A.M. BRIEFING AT 7:00 A.M. OFF TO THE CONTINENT FOR A SIGHT
SEEING TOUR (RUBBER-NECK MISSION). OF GERMANY FOR GROUND TROOPS.
I GOT MY SHIP STUCK IN MUD AND HAD TO CHANGE. MY SHIP WAS SCRUBBED DUE TO
LATE TAKE OFF. WE WERE TO PICK UP OUR PASSENGERS AT ALKENBERY. (THEY ARE
GROUND CREW FOR THE PEA SHOOTERS).
REMAINDER OF DAY QUITE PEACEFUL FOR ALL CONCERNED.

From the diary of Lt. Phil Darby:

Played tennis this morning and 18 holes on Royston course with Marty and Cooper.

==

MAY 11
BREAKFAST AT 8:00 BRIEFING AT 8:30. MISSION TO LENZ, AUSTRIA TO FLY OUT ALLIED
PRISONERS OF WAR TO EITHER FRANCE (FRENCHMEN AND AMERICANS) OR ENGLAND
(LIMMIES). THEY RAN OUT OF P.W.'S BEFORE THEY DID SHIPS SO WE CAME HOME EMPTY.
SAW MANY HALF-STARVED PEOPLE. ACTUALLY THEY WERE JUST SKIN AND BONE. SOME
BARELY ABLE TO WALK. KITTY GAVE ONE OLD MAN SOME BACON AND HE CRIED AND
KISSED HIS HAND OVER AND OVER. THE FIELD WE LANDED ON WAS QUITE GOOD
CONDITION BUT IN MANY PLACES THE GROUND WAS RED WITH BLOOD. WE FLEW A
TOTAL OF 1400 MILES TO DAY[sic] IN 9:20 HRS[sic] WITH OUT[sic] GETTING ANY THING
ACCOMPLISHED. WE FLEW AT 2000 FT AND SAW THE RESULTS OF OUR LABOR. GERMAN
TOWNS ARE IN COMPLETE RUINS. TODAY WE GOT FLAK AT DUNKIRK !!

From the diary of Lt. Phil Darby:

Flew to Lenz, Austria, south of Prague to pick up some liberated P.O.W.'s. Most of the planes were loaded with French Officers, but we came back empty. Austria is a very pretty country. Lenz is on the Danube, which wasn't so blue today. We tried talking to a Pole who was a slave laborer. We also gave him some of our K-ration food. The Germans we saw are starved and homeless - also, shocked. They can't realize the war is over.

==

MAY 12
MORNING MEETING. WENT TO BIG "C" FOR FITTING OF BATTLE JACKET. TWO WEEKS LATE ON FITTING NOW. GOT TO BASE AT 1230.

From the diary of Lt. Phil Darby:

Golf with Coop then beer and sandwiches at Bull Hotel in Royston.

==

MAY 13
BREAKFAST AT 12:45 A.M. BRIEFING AT 1:15 A.M. OFF TO STETTIN, GERMANY FOR MORE PRISONERS OF WAR. IT TURNS OUT MANY MEN GOT NO SLEEP LAST NIGHT. FLEW 31 P.W.'S FROM BARTH (NEAR STETTIN) TO A-70 (NEAR ORLEANS). MANY OF THE MEN HAD BEEN P.W.'S FOR OVER TWO YEARS. THEY WERE A BATCH OF HAPPY BOYS. WHEN WE GOT HOME WE WENT THRU A DE-LOUSEING PROCESS. TOTAL TIME FLYING WAS 9:40 HRS. LANDED HOME BASE[sic] AT 1500 HOURS. THE SACK IS VERY INVITING TO DAY[sic] SINCE AT THIS TIME I HAVE HAD NO SLEEP FOR THE PAST 40 HOURS.

From the diary of Lt. Phil Darby:

We landed at Barth, Germany and took on 31 Amer. P.O.W.s It is near Stettin and Keil; close to the Polish border. We flew them to A-70 (France). There we[re] a happy bunch of boys.

==

MAY 14
REGULAR MORNING MEETING AGAIN.

PERSONAL PROCEESSING[sic] IN THE P.M.

EARLY TO BED AGAIN IN HOPES OF GETTIN' RID OF MY COLD.

==

153

MAY 15
REGULAR MORNING MEETING. FLEW A CAMERA BOMBING MISSION WITH LT. RABER IN
P.M. [bombardier]

AT 1300 HOURS WE HAS AN EQUIPMENT CHECK AND ISSUE OF ALL SHORTAGES. TO-
DAY[sic] WE WERE TOLD (1500 HRS) THAT WE ALL WOULD BE HOME BY THE END OF JUNE.
THE GROUP WILL HAVE GONE FROM BASSINGBOURN BY 10 JUNE. GROUP IS TO BECOME A
TRAINING UNIT IN THE STATES. THE MEN WITH THE FEWER MISSIONS WILL FLY HOME
WHILE THE GROUP VETERANS WILL GO BY BOAT. 40 SHIPS ARE TO LEAVE FOR THE STATES
IN 4 DAYS. SEEMS BOAT RIDE IS BEST DEAL !

===

MAY 16
THEY SAY THAT MY CREW IS GOING TO FLY HOME. IN ORDER TO FLY HOME WE MUST
MEET A.T.C. REQUIREMENTS: 20 HRS. INSTRUMENTS; 7 HR. CELESTIAL NIGHT NAVIGATION;
8 HR. DAY CELESTIAL NAV.

TODAY WE FLEW 11 HOURS - 5 HRS IN P.M. THEN FLEW ALL NIGHT TO CONTINENT. LOTS OF
HARD WORK AND LONG HOURS BUT WORTH IT ! WE WERE OVER FRANCE IN OVERCAST AT
15000' WHEN OUR AIR SPEED INDICATOR FROZE UP. WE WERE FORTUNATE - IT THAWED
OUT AFTER A WHILE AT A LOWER ALTITUDE.

===

MAY 17
WE LANDED THIS A.M. AT 6 A.M. AND GOT TO BED ABOUT 7 A.M. AT 11:15A.M. CAPT WARD
GOT US UP TO FLY AT 1315. WE HAVE BEEN FLYING ALL P.M.
EARLY TO BED AGAIN TONITE[sic]

===

MAY 18
BREAKFAST AT 7:15; BRIEFING AT 8:00. TAKE OFF TO FLY DAY NAVIGATION MISSION
CROSS COUNTRY (8 HOURS). THIS SHOULD COMPLETE OUR A.T.C. REQUIREMENTS. GOT
LOTS OF ACTUAL INSTRUMENTS AGAIN TODAY.
EARLY TO BED AGAIN.

===

MAY 19
WENT TO SICK CALL - HAVE AN INFECTION OF RIGHT EAR DUE TO WEARING OF HEADSET.

SPENT QUIET AND PEACEFUL DAY FOR A CHANGE.

ALL FLYING OFFICERS AND MEN RESTRICTED TO BASE AND WERE GIVEN A 64 (PHYSICAL
EXAM) TODAY.

EARLY TO BED AGAIN TONITE !

===

MAY 20
TODAY IS A DAY OF REST SO THEY GOT US UP AT 9 A.M. TO FLY TEST HOPS. (GAS
CONSUMPTION CHECKS). WE FLEW IN BAD WEATHER AND LANDED ABOUT 1400 HRS.
BIG PARTY (BY GROUPE) TONITE[sic]. BEER SELLS FOR HALF-PENNY (1-CENT) AND
WHISKEY FOR SIX PENCE (10-CENTS) ! SHOULD TURN OUT TO BECOME A BIG BLOW OUT !

===

MAY 21
PEACE FUL[sic] DAY AND NO FLYING FOR ME THIS DAY.

ONE OF GROUPE OF CREWS ARE ALERTED TO RETURN TO THE STATES.

EARLY TO BED FOR LITTLE SLEEP

===

MAY 22
WENT TO BIG "C" FOR BATTLE JACKETS AND RETURNED IN TIME TO FLY A FERRY SHIP TO
THURLIEGH. A TOTAL OF 15 SHIPS (ALL IN THE GROUP) ARE TRANSFERED TO ANOTHER
GROUPE. THREE CREWS TAKE OFF FOR STATES AT 11 A.M.

[Information in Marion H. Havelaar's The Ragged Irregulars of Bassingbourn - The 91st Bombgroup in
World War II, indicates that the "Out House Mouse" is NOT one of the transferred aircraft - grh]

===

MAY 23
MORNING MEETING. ALL EXCESS EQUIPMENT TURNED IN TO SUPPLY TODAY.

WAS TO FLY IN A.M. BUT HAD OIL LEAK IN #1 ENGINE ON TAKE OFF AND HAD TO LAND. UP
TO FLY AGAIN IN P.M. BUT DID NOT DUE TO #3 TURBO RUNAWAY.

===

MAY 24
WAS TO LEAVE FOR U.S.A. THIS DAY BUT DATE CHANGED AGAIN. GOLLY, WE SHOULD
MAKE IT SOON.

===

155

MAY 25
SEE 7 JUNE 1945

THESE DAYS [between May 25 and June 7] SPENT WASTEING[sic] TIME UNTIL THE "WHEELS"
DECIDED WHEN TO SEND US HOME !

===

JUNE 7
ALERTED TO LEAVE FOR UNITED STATES ON THE MORROW.

EARLY TO BED AGAIN !

===

JUNE 8
BREAKFAST AT 4:15, BRIEFING AT 5:15. TAKE OFF AT 7:15. TAKE OFF TIME SET BACK TO
8:15. DESTINATION IS VALLEY, ENGLAND, AN A.T.C. BASE FOR TRIP ACROSS THE ATLANTIC
OCEAN. LANDED AT VALLEY AT 10:30 A.M. HAD LUNCH, BRIEFING AT 2:30 FOR LEG OVER
WATER TO MEEKS FLD, ICELAND. TAKE OFF AT 1800 HRS. LOTS OF CLOUDS AND
INSTRUMENT FLYING. FEATHER #2 ENGINE 3 HRS OUT OF MEEKS, DUE TO BROKEN LINE ON
GOVONOR[sic]. HAD TO MAKE INSTRUMENT LET-DOWN AND MADE 3 PASSES AT THE FIELD
DUE TO LOW CEILINGS. LANDED AT 0130, 9 JUNE.

[See note of June 11. Lt. Harvey's crew is NOT flying "Out House Mouse". As anyone who has skied on a
cloudy day can attest, it is very difficult to distinguish the ground and its features when the snow, ice and
clouds all blend together from the lack of light and shadows from the sun. – grh]

===

JUNE 9
LANDED MEEKS AT 1:30 A.M. GOT 3 HRS SLEEP THEN - BREAKFAST AT 04:00, BRIEFING AT
5:00. TAKE OFF A[t] 07:00. TAKE OFF HELD UP DUE TO MAINTANACE [sic] OF #2 ENGINE.
TAKE OFF FINALLY AT 1200 FOR GOOSE BAY, LABRADOR.
GOOD WEATHER MOST OF WAY. LANDED AT GOOSE BAY AT 21:40. WE REMAINED OVER
NITE [sic] AND ALL THE CREW (10 MEN) AND PASSENGERS (10 MEN) WERE VERY THANKFUL
FOR A CHANCE TO SLEEP AND CLEAN UP.

[A B-17 is not that big an airplane and is certainly not configured to take passengers. It must have been very
crowded in the waist area that usually had only 3-men but is now carrying at least 13 – its usual 3 plus the 10
passengers. This assumes that all the other crew members are in their normal flight positions. – grh]

===

JUNE 10
BRIEFING AT 1400 HRS. TAKE OFF AT 1630.
LOW CEILINGS ALL THE WAY TO DESTINATION. WE WERE SENT TO LAND AT GRENIER FLD,
NEW HAMPSHIRE IN STEAD[sic] OF BRADLEY FLD, CONN AS PLANNED DUE TO BAD
WEATHER. WE REMAINED AT GRENIER OVER NITE[sic] AND MADE PHONE CALLS MOST OF
THE NITE [sic]. CALLED MARIBELLE IN EVENING.

From the diary of Lt. Phil Darby:

Flew B-17G "Lewd Angel" home (USA) from England

==

JUNE 11
TAKE OFF FROM GRENIER FLD FOR BRADLEY FLD, CONN. AT 1550 AND ARRIVED AT
DESTINATION AT 16:30. HOME AT LAST AND HERE WE GOT MILK FOR THE FIRST TIME
SINCE LEAVING U.S.A.

[NOTE:
When they disembarked at Grenier Field it marked the last time any of the crew would fly a combat B-17.
Per George Odenwaller, Lt. Harvey's crew did NOT fly the "Out House Mouse" home despite the personal
request and/or complaint of Lt. Harvey. Being of the "Old Army" this action would have been very unusual
for Lt. Harvey and emphasizes his desire to return to the US in his assigned aircraft. Lt. Darby's diary states
they returned in the "B-17G 'Lewd Angel'", while George Odenwaller stated in some notes he sent me that
"We flew home as a crew in 'Incendiary Blonde', #44-6591, LG-U a 322nd B.S. A/C. Landed at Bradly
Field, U.S.A." "Incendiary Blonde" was also a B-17-G and both aircraft were unpainted.

Plane Names & Fancy Noses, states on pages 116-117 that "Lewd Angel" was recalled 3-1/2 hours out from
Wales to Burtonwood due a suspected flat tire suffered during take-off from Valley. The delay would no
doubt have been noteworthy.   On page 99 in the history of "Incendiary Blond" the same source states that
"Finally on 8th June, along with many other heavy bombers from the group, it took off from Valley in Wales
and began the long flight back to the USA with a crew of ten, plus another ten passengers." This passenger
and crew count agrees with Lt. Harvey's entry of June 9.

According to the aircraft record from Plane Names & Fancy Noses, the "Out House Mouse" returned to the
USA on May 25 so she beat her last combat crew home.

It is unfortunate that with such remarkable war records, both the "Nine-O-Nine" and the "Out House Mouse"
were unable to avoid the cutting torches while at the aircraft graveyard outside of Kingman, Arizona. It is
believed the "Out House Mouse" survived until 1963.

However, while the original aircraft are gone, their remarkable histories will live on. Tom Reilly and his
organization have already restored a flying replica of the "Nine-O-Nine" and are nearing completion on their
reconstruction of the "Out House Mouse" – grh]

==

JUNE 12
PROCESSED AT BRADLEY FLD AND LEFT FOR CAMP MILES STANDISH [later referred to as CMS - grh] MASS. LEFT BRADLEY AT 0800 AND GOT INTO CMS[sic] AT 1300. PROCESSED AGAIN AND BEGAIN[sic] OUR WAIT FOR TRAINS OUT TO NEXT STOP.

==

JUNE 13
STILL SWEATIN' OUT TRANSPORTATION TO NEXT STOP ! CALLED MARIBELLE IN EVENING.

==

JUNE 14
LEFT CMS[sic] FOR JEFFERSON BARRACKS [later referred to as J.B. - grh] AT 1345. WE WENT BY TROOP TRAIN WHICH WAS A DIRTY COACH CARS. [sic]

==

JUNE 15
STILL ON TRAIN FOR J.B. [Jefferson Barracks – grh] DUE INTO ST. LOUIS AT 1830 HOURS. FINALLY MADE IT AT 2100 HRS:

NOTE OF INTEREST:
IT TOOK US 30+45 HRS TO GO FROM C.M.S TO J.B. WHILE IT ONLY TOOK 26 HOURS TO FLY FROM MIDDLE OF ENGLAND TO BRADLY[sic] CONN. A DISTANCE OF ABOUT 4500 MILES !

==

JUNE 16
PROCESSED AT 7:30 AND OFF FOR BOONE, IOWA AT 1200. ZEPHER TO LEAVE ST. LOUIS AT 1700. DUE IN CEDAR RAPIDS AT 1255. HAD ONLY WOOL CLOTHES TO WEAR SINCE ALL COTTONS ARE SOLD OUT IN ST. LOUIS ! 30 DAY LEAVE EFFECTIVE TODAY. REPORT BACK TO J.B. 19 JULY.

==

JUNE 17
STILL ON TRAIN. DUE TO FLOODS TRAIN HAD TO DETOUR. AT BURLINGTON DEVELOPED "HOT BOX" TROUBLE AND FINALLY MADE IT TO CEDAR RAPIDS AT 0430. A TOTAL OF 11-1/2 HRS ON THE "FAST" ZEPHER. TRAIN TO BOONE GONE. TOOK BUS TO BOONE AT 6:25 AND GOT HOME AT 1300 HRS.

HOME AGAIN !!!!

==

JUNE 18
LEAVE

==

JUNE 19
CARL REMY CAME TO VISIT FROM CALIFORNIA. FIRST TIME HE HAS SEEN ANNE AND BOB.

[This is the last daily entry in the diary. Even July 19 is blank. Apparently, these orders were changed due to the progress being made at that time in the Pacific against Japan.   World War II finally ended September 2, 1945 with the formal surrender of Japan. - grh]

==

[The following notations are found on the very last page of Lt. Harvey's diary - grh]

       FLYING TRAINING
AUG 1943   JAN 1945
PREFLIGHT: 10 WEEKS COURSE
    SEA & AIR RECOGNITION   30 HRS.
    CODE 48 HRS; PHYSICS, 24 HRS; MATH 20 HRS
    MAPS & CHARTS 18 HRS; DAILY PHYSICAL TNG.
PRIMARY: 10 WEEKS; 70 HRS FLYING;
    94 HRS ACADEMIC WORK; 54 HRS MIL[i]TARY TNG.
BASIC; 10 WEEKS: 70 HRS FLYING; 94 HRS
    GROUND SCHOOL; 47 HOURS MILITARY TNG.
ADVANCED; 10 WEEKS; 70 HRS FLYING;
    60 HRS GROUND SCHOOL; 19 HRS MILT. TNG.
TRANSITION; 10 WEEKS; 105 HOURS FLYING
    REMAINDER GROUND SCHOOL
PHASES; 12 WEEKS; 150 HRS FLYING
    REMAINDER GROUND SCHOOL.

==

[End of Lt. Harvey's diary - grh]

==

[This page intentionally left blank]

A Scrap Book
and
Photograph Album
from
The Crew

Im Westen:

Nach Rundstedts Verzweiflungsoffensive:

Sturm auf den Westwall

Fast 900 000 deutsche Gefangene seit der Invasion

Anglo-amerikanische Luftoffensive

vom Westwall bis zur Ostfront

Im Osten:

Schlesien, die „Ruhr des Ostens", verloren

Sächsisches Industriegebiet bedroht

Ostpreussen überrannt

Schukows Armeen vor Berlin

WG. 37.

The front side of a "Nickle" or Allied propaganda leaflet. This particular one was printed heavy black type on a red tissue-like paper.

A subjective translation is:
"In the west, 900,000 Germans have been taken prisoner since the invasion,
In the east, East Prussia is overrun and General Zhukov's Red Army is at Berlin"

Ergebnis der Krim-Konferenz

ZWISCHEN PREMIERMINISTER CHURCHILL, PRÄSIDENT ROOSEVELT UND MARSCHALL STALIN

Antwort auf Deutschlands Schicksalsfrage:

Nazi-Deutschland ist zum Untergang verurteilt. Fortsetzung des aussichtslosen Widerstandes heisst, dass das deutsche Volk die Niederlage noch schwerer zu bezahlen haben wird.

ES IST NICHT DAS ZIEL DER ALLIIERTEN, DAS DEUTSCHE VOLK ZU VER-NICHTEN. Aber erst nach der Ausrottung des Nationalsozialismus und des Militarismus wird das deutsche Volk auf ein anständiges Dasein und auf einen Platz in der Gemeinschaft der Völker hoffen können.

Besetzung und Kontrolle Deutschlands:

Die drei Grossmächte werden je eine Zone Deutschlands besetzen, die von einer Zentral-Kontrollkommission, bestehend aus den Oberbefehlshabern der drei Grossmächte, mit dem Sitz in Berlin, einheitlich verwaltet und kontrolliert werden. Frankreich wird aufgefordert, die Besetzung einer eigenen Zone zu übernehmen.

Um dafür zu sorgen, dass Deutschland nie wieder den Frieden der Welt stören kann, werden folgende Massnahmen getroffen:

Entwaffnung und Auflösung der Wehrmacht;

Auflösung des deutschen Generalstabs;

Ausmerzung oder Kontrolle aller wehrwirtschaftlich wichtigen Industrien; schnelle Aburteilung aller Kriegsverbrecher;

Wiedergutmachung aller von Deutschland verursachten Schäden durch Sachleistungen;

Austilgung der NSDAP, ihrer Gesetze, Organisationen und Einrichtungen;

Ausmerzung jedes nationalsozialistischen oder militaristischen Einflusses bei Behörden und im Kultur- und Wirtschaftsleben Deutschlands; jede Massnahme, die für die Sicherung des künftigen Friedens der Welt notwendig erscheint.

Wiedergutmachung:

Auf welche Weise und in welchem Ausmass Deutschland den Schaden wieder gutzumachen hat, den es den Alliierten zugefügt hat, wird von einer Wiedergutmachungskommission entschieden werden, die ihren Sitz in Moskau hat.

Über den beträchtlichen Gebietszuwachs, den Polen im Norden und Westen erhalten muss, wird die Friedenskonferenz entscheiden.

Welt-Einigkeit im Frieden wie im Kriege

Durch Fortsetzung und Ausbau der Zusammenarbeit und des Verständnisses zwischen unseren drei Völkern kann das höchste Streben der Menschheit verwirklicht werden — ein sicherer und dauerhafter Friede, der, in den Worten der Atlantik-Charter, „eine Gewähr dafür bietet, dass alle Menschen in allen Ländern frei von Furcht und Not werden leben können."

The reverse side of the "Nickle" printed in traditional black on white.

General translation is that as a result of the Crime Conference, the three super powers will divide Germany into three sections with Berlin as the seat of power. Other topics include the need to weed out Nationalists and military from the German population and the need to make war reparations.

Я американец

"Ya Amerikánets" *(Pronounced as spelt)*

Пожалуйста сообщите сведения обо мне в Американскую Военную Миссию в Москве	Please communicate my particulars to American Military Mission Moscow

For missions over Slavic territory, these American flags and "I am an American" printed in Russian were part of their survival equipment. The instructions are on the facing page.

INSTRUCTIONS

(1) Learn by heart the Russian phrase "Ya Amerikánets" (*means "I am American" and is pronounced as spelt*).

(2) Carry this folder and contents in left breast pocket.

(3) If you have time before contact with Russian troops, take out the folder and attach it (*flag side outwards*) to front of pocket.

(4) When spotted by Russian troops put up your hands holding the flag in one of them and call out the phrase "Ya Amerikánets."

(5) If you are spotted before taking action as at para 3 do **NOT** attempt to extract folder or flag. Put up your hands and call out phrase "Ya Amerikánets." The folder will be found when you are searched.

(6) You must understand that these recognition aids **CANNOT** be accepted by Soviet troops as proof of bona fides as they may be copied by the enemy. They should however protect you until you are cross questioned by competent officers.

The instructions for the "I am an American" survival notice which was folded with an American flag on one side and the Russian, "I am an American" on the other were carried in a small vinyl case in the left pocket of their flight suit.

165

Bassingbourn, England

Courtesy W.M. Limberger

This aerial view of Bassingbourn made during 1943 shows all of the old base except for some of the plane dispersal areas. This was a mighty sweet sight after a rough ride to Germany or wherever.

[The control tower can be seen in the center of the picture with two hangers on either side. Left to right, the hanger are: 322 BS, 323 BS, (tower), 324 BS, 401 BS. The tower is now a museum. – grh]

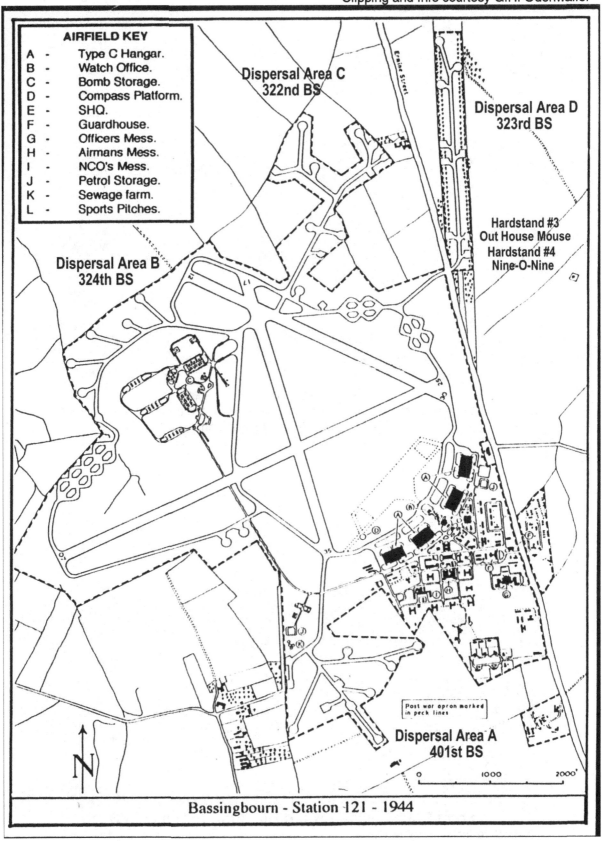

AIRFIELD KEY

A - Type C Hangar.
B - Watch Office.
C - Bomb Storage.
D - Compass Platform.
E - SHQ.
F - Guardhouse.
G - Officers Mess.
H - Airmans Mess.
I - NCO's Mess.
J - Petrol Storage.
K - Sewage farm.
L - Sports Pitches.

Dispersal Area C
322nd BS

Dispersal Area D
323rd BS

Hardstand #3
Out House Mouse
Hardstand #4
Nine-O-Nine

Dispersal Area B
324th BS

Dispersal Area A
401st BS

Post war apron marked
in peck lines

0   1000   2000'

N

Bassingbourn - Station 121 - 1944

167

View from Control Tower
[Unpainted B-17's are most likely the newer G models. Near the center is seen a P-47 and to the far left a newer P-51 fighter airplane – grh]

Front Gate looking toward Huntingdon-Royston Road
(Distinctive "horseshoe" road that can be seen in aerial photos is just in the foreground - grh)

Nose Art and Mission Markers – Out House Mouse
[Using its nose art, the identity of the next aircraft back is "Ramblin Rebel" - grh]

Out House Mouse on its Bombing Run

View from inside the Ball Turret – George's foot is in upper left

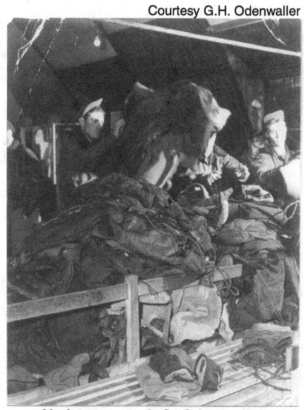

**N. Jorgenson & G. Odenwaller
Turning in Equipment after a Mission**

Back, L-R: 2nd Lt. Paul Katz, Navigator; 1st Lt. Elmer "Joe" Harvey, Pilot;
2nd Lt. Phil Darby, Co-pilot
Front, L-R: S/Sgt. Niel Jorgenson, Engineer; S/Sgt. Milton Lloyd, Radio;
S/Sgt. George H. Odenwaller, Ball Turret Gunner;
S/Sgt. Walter Limberger, Tail Gunner

[Photo by Al Kus, date is unknown. - grh]

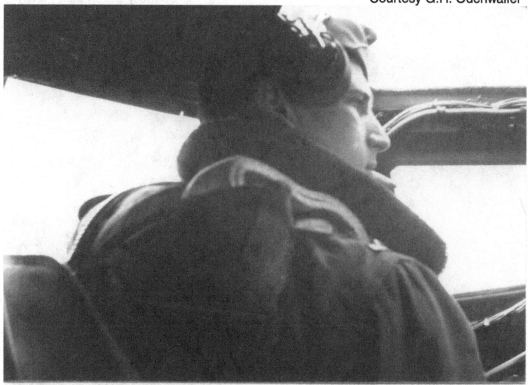

Lt. E. J. "Joe" Harvey – Pilot

Lt. Phil "Rock" Darby – Co-Pilot

Lt. Marty "Radar" Raber – Bombardier

Lt. Paul "Files" Katz – Navigator
[Toggelier" in background is unidentified - grh]

S/Sgt. Niel "Jorgy" Jorgenson – Flight Engineer

S/Sgt. George "Dutch" Odenwaller – Ball Turret Gunner
[Many crews "personalized" their aircraft by painting the sweethearts name near their position - grh]

S/Sgt. Allen E. Kus
Waist Gunner

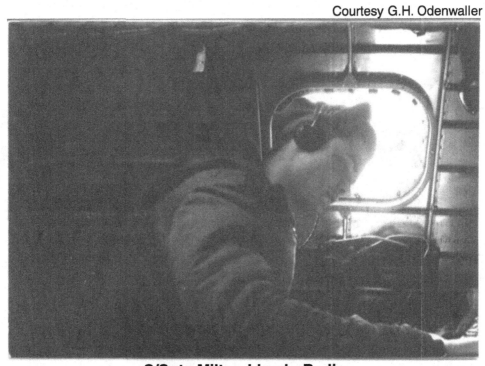

S/Sgt. Milton Lloyd - Radio
[Sporting his flak vest & Clark Cable mustache - grh]

 Courtesy W.M. Limberger

S/Sgt. Walter "Lindy" Limberger – Tail Gunner
[The long and narrow taper after the gunner's window identifies it as an original B-17 tail – grh]

Composite by grh

A look through the cockpit door

Photo shows part of ground crew.
Names of full crew: M/Sgt. Rollin L. Davis, Robert M. Waddell, Edward J. Lincoln,
Cpl. Charles H. Huffman, Cpl. Albert A. McLaughlin, Nicholas V. Palma-Ball, Sgt. Emil M Yezdimer

'Nine-O-Nine' is Tops in Maintenance

DAVIS　　YEZDIMER　　WADDELL　　LINCOLN　　HUFFMAN　　McLAUGHLIN

By Sid Schapiro
Stars and Stripes Staff Writer

The Fortress Nine-O-Nine, which terminated its operational career in the ETO two weeks before VE-Day, is 8th Air Force heavy-bomber maintenance champion—completing 140 consecutive missions in 13 months without a turnback for mechanical reasons.

M/Sgt. Rollin L. Davis, of Miles, Tex., who holds the Bronze Star with cluster, is ground-crew chief, assisted by Sgts. Emil M. Yezdimer, of Philadelphia; Robert M. Waddell, of Rushtown, Ohio, and Edward J. Lincoln Jr., of Damariscotta Mills, Me.; Cpls. Charles H. Huffman, of Missoula, Mont., and Albert A. McLaughlin, of Kilgore, Tex.

Flying with the veteran 91st Bomb Group of the 1st Air Division, the Nine-

O-Nine made its first combat trip on Mar. 2, 1944, hit the century mark on Jan. 15, 1945, and racked up No. 140 on Apr. 25, participating in attacks on every major German target, including 18 trips to Berlin. Four complete crews finished tours of operations on Nine-O-Nine, which underwent 27 engine changes.

Davis is looking forward to flying back to the U.S. in Nine-O-Nine, and then going to the Pacific, where he hopes to do as good a maintenance job on B29s.

Runners-up for top maintenance honors were the 447th Bomb Group's Fortress Milk Wagon with 129 missions and the 467th Bomb Group's Liberator Witchcraft with 128 combat trips—without an abort. However, Witchcraft and Milk Wagon led the 2nd and 3rd Air Divisions respectively.

A recipient of the Bronze Star and

cluster, as well as a commendation by Gen. Carl A. Spaatz, USSTAF commander, M/Sgt. Jose R. Ramirez, of Los Angeles, is Witchcraft's ground-crew chief. Ramirez, who is of Mexican stock, and his four assistants comprise a heterogeneous group, representing five nationalities.

S/Sgt. George Y. Dong, of Coronado, Cal., assistant crew chief, is of Chinese descent. Sgt. Raymond A. Betcher, of Mt. Clemens, Mich., and Cpl. Joseph J. Vetter, of Merrick, N.Y., are of Dutch and German parentage respectively, while Cpl. Walter L. Elliott, of St. Louis claims only American ancestry.

The Milk Wagon's ground-crew chief is T/Sgt. Robert Orlosky, of Brockway, Pa. S/Sgt. Harlan Armes, of Petros, Tenn., is assistant crew chief.

[This same ground crew also serviced the "Out House Mouse" during its 139 missions. – grh]

Casual Moments at Bassingbourn

Phil Darby & Marty Raber – "2-Clowns"

Phil Darby

Marty Raber

Paul Katz (sneezing) & Joe Harvey
[Mrs. Katz said that Paul's sneeze always made everyone laugh - grh]

Paul Katz
Joe Harvey

**M. Lloyd & N. Jorgenson
With "Hi Ho Silver" (130 Missions)**

G. Odenwaller and W. Limberger

N. Jorgenson, G. Odenwaller, A. Kus & M. Lloyd

W. Limberger, A. Kus, M. Lloyd & N. Jorgenson

George Odenwaller
[Note his hand-painted 91st Bomb Group Insignia on his jacket - grh]

**W. Limberger in his A-2 Jacket
Painted by G. Odenwaller**

George Odenwaller & Al Kus
Sporting the usual "Base Casual" attire

Niel Jorgenson leaving the Mess Hall

Walter Limberger

Al Kus

Walter & The April 30, 1945 - Snow !!

**Photo of Walter Limberger's Painting
"The Mouse and The Flea"
by Jerry Crandall**

Frankfurt　　　　**Headlines of**　　　　**Paris**
The Stars and Stripes

A collage of 33 photographs of Europe on VE-Day
from the destruction in Germany to the surviving beauty of Paris …

... And a reminder of what it cost.

As They Are Now

Courtesy W.M. Limberger

91st Bomb Group Reunion – Savannah, Ga. – 1998

Standing (L-R): Joan and Paul Katz (glasses); Mrs. John Krumm; George Odenwaller (hand raised)
Seated (L-R): Marty and Marilyn Raber; Phil and Doris Darby; Eve Odenwaller
Photo by John Krumm – Brother-in-Law of Geo & Eve Odenwaller

(At the time of this photo, only Lt. Joe Harvey and S/Sgt Niel Jorgenson are deceased – grh)

And After the War?

1Lt. Elmer "Joe" Harvey – Pilot
Lt Harvey was one of the two married officers during his ETO tour. After the war, he and his small family moved to Iowa City, Iowa where he obtained his B.A. degree in Business Administration from the University of Iowa. Following graduation, he entered the retail ready-to-wear business as a buyer of women's coats and dresses for Younker Brothers Department stores in Des Moines, Iowa. During his career he and his family lived in Des Moines, Iowa; Denver, Colorado; Minneapolis, Minnesota; and Suffern, New York. His descendants number 4 children (2-boys and 2-girls), 4 grandchildren (1-boy and 3-girls), and one great-granddaughter. He died in March 1972 of heart failure.

2Lt. Phil. N. Darby – Co-Pilot
Lt Darby first attended Washington University in St. Louis, Missouri and received his B.S. degree in Natural Sciences and then went on to obtain his M.A. degree in English Literature from the University of Nebraska at Lincoln, Nebraska. In 1950, he and his family moved to Los Angeles, California where he pursued his career in Pharmaceutical Sales with the Parke-Davis and Dupont Companies. Retired in 1991, he has 3-children (2-boys and 1-girl) and 4 grandchildren (2-boys and 2-girls). He currently lives in Fillmore, California.

2Lt. Martin J. Raber – Bombardier
Upon his return to the United States, Lt. Raber entered Med-School at St. Johns College in Brooklyn, New York and served his internship in Osteopathic Medicine in Philadelphia, Pennsylvania. For 35-years he practiced family medicine in Hawthorne, New Jersey. Retired in 1986, the Rabers' have 2-children (1-boy and 1-girl) and 5-grandchildren (4-boys and 1-girl). They currently live in Ho Ho Kus, New Jersey.

2Lt. Paul Katz – Navigator
Lt. Katz was the other married officer during his ETO tour. After the war, he attended New York University where he obtained his B.S degree in Accounting. A year later, he obtained his certification as a Certified Public Accountant. During his career he worked for the Army Audit Agency, Litton Industries, Sun Chemical and the Kollsman Instrument Company noted for their aircraft altimeters which are part of the instrumentation used on the Space Shuttle. In 1978 the Katz's moved to California where Paul opened his own accounting business. While his wife Joan says that he never really stopped working, he "retired" in 1979. They have 2-daughters and 1-granddaughter. Paul died of heart failure March 12, 1999.

S/Sgt. Niel C. Jorgenson – Engineer & Top Turret
S/Sgt Jorgenson returned home to Salt Lake City to work as a civilian aircraft mechanic at Hill Air Force Base, Utah. His daughter said he could fix anything. Following his retirement in 1966, he kept active by working in the family jewelry store; as a mechanic at the golf course and by traveling. Niel is survived by his 2-children (1-boy and 1-girl) and 4-grandchildren (1-boy and 3-girls). Niel died of a stroke in 1982.

S/Sgt. George H. Odenwaller – Ball Turret Gunner
S/Sgt Odenwaller spent his first 47-years after the war working as a professional model maker. These are the men who provide industries and corporations with the full size mock-up models of whatever their next product might be. During his career, George made models ranging in size from a travel alarm clock the size of a quarter to a full size mock-up of the proposed interior of the Boeing 707 aircraft. Some of the companies he mentioned are the Ford Motor Company, Kohner Brothers and Topper Toys. He was a supervisor at Proto-Type Models for 26 years retiring "under protest" in 1995. George and his wife have 2-children (1-boy and 1-girl) and continue to live in New Jersey.

S/Sgt. Milton H. Lloyd – Radio

S/Sgt. Lloyd returned to his hometown of Omaha, Nebraska and attended Creighton University where he obtained both his B.A. and M.A. degrees in Chemistry. Due to his interest in radio-activity, after graduation he went to work in the Chemical Technology Division of the Oak Ridge National Laboratory in Oak Ridge, Tennessee. After 31 years, he retired as Senior Research Chemist and Group Leader. His immediate family consists of 1-boy and 2-girls followed by 4-grandchildren (2-boys and 2-girls) and 2-great grandchildren (2-boys). Milton still lives in Oak Ridge, Tennessee.

S/Sgt. Elmer "Al" Kus – Waist Gunner/Spot Jammer

S/Sgt. Kus returned to Illinois and studied Architectural Engineering at Armor Institute of Technology (now ITT). Upon graduation, he worked as a draftsman and ultimately an engineer. In 1978, he started his own company, Kustom Construction Company in Lombard, Illinois where he continues to work today. Al has 3-children (1-boy and 2-girls) and 9-grandchildren (5-boys and 4-girls). He currently lives in Oak Brook, Illinois.

S/Sgt. Walter M. Limberger – Tail Gunner

S/Sgt. Limberger really wanted to stay in the military and cross-train into weather; however the Army, in their own way, said they no longer had need for gunners so Walter took up transports where he gained experience driving large tanker trucks refueling the B-29's in Savannah, Georgia. When he was separated from the service, this experience helped him obtain employment driving "P&D" (pick-up and deliver) and long-haul trucks for the Teamsters. In 1986 he retired after 40-years but still maintains his status as a retired member of Local 671 in East Hartford, Connecticut. He must have been able to juggle his long-haul driving and his family well, for Walter has the largest family of all of his fellow crew members numbering 9-children (5-boys and 4-girls), 17-grandchildren and 7-great grandchildren. Walter now lives in Vernon, Connecticut.

A BRIEF HISTORY OF THE B-17 KNOWN AS THE "OUT HOUSE MOUSE"

* Airframe number 42-31636, is the fourth of 100 aircraft (42-31632 – 42-31731) built by Boeing in block B-17G-25-BO where "BO" refers to Boeing and "42" refers to the year of the contract. The first Boeing B-17G was 42-31032, in block B-17G-1-BO, making this the 604th of a total of 4,035 B-17G's produced by Boeing and 8,680 in all. On November 26, 1943 she was added to the Army inventory.

* Originally she is assigned to the 457th Bomb Group at Wendover, Utah, December 11, 1943. The 457th Bomb Group was deployed to Glatton, England by way of Newfoundland and Greenland and arrived in England January 20, 1944. The aircraft was transferred to the 323rd Bomb Squadron, 91st Bomb Group, on March 12, 1944.

* At that time she is apparently still unnamed. There is no record of when and how she received her name but quite likely she may have been named by Bill Reid, Operations Officer of the 323rd. When Bill was in his teens, his mother Edythe, often said that Bill was "as wild and crazy as an outhouse mouse". Her figure of speech may have became the inspiration for the name of the B-17 that achieved the second best combat record of the entire 8th Air Force with 139 combat missions – second only to her sister ship, the "Nine-O-Nine", with 140 missions.
    As with many of the aircraft at Bassingbourn, her nose art is the work of Tony Starcer who based the mouse on Jerry Mouse of the "Tom and Jerry" cartoons. [I suspect that most diary references to the aircraft by name show it as "Out House Mouse" due to the slanted "T" in the word "out" on the nose-art which makes the name appear as three words. Most book references give the name as two words – "Outhouse Mouse". Two words or three, it is the same aircraft. – grh]

* During the August 16th, 1944 mission to the Siebel aircraft factory at Halle, the aircraft is said to have been the first heavy bomber to be attacked by the German, jet powered Me-163 Komet airplane. While page 159 of <u>Plane Names and Fancy Noses</u>, by Ray Bowden gives a description of the attack and the famous painting known as "The Mouse and The Flea" by Jerry Crandall clearly depicts OR-N #636 during the event, Mr. Lowell Getz, in his book, <u>"Mary Ruth" – Memories of Mobile…We Still Remember,</u> Page 119, indicates that the actual aircraft was "Betty Lou's Buggy". Mr. Getz's sources include the August 16th Interrogation Forms from the debriefings of the aircrews obtained from the National Archives. These show that Lt. Walter R. Mullins was in #579 ("Betty Lou's Buggy") and Lt. James E. Faris was in #636 ("Out House Mouse"). With major damage from an attack of 25 FW-190's and the loss of two superchargers, Lt. Mullins had to jettison his bomb load and leave the formation before the I.P. About 50 minutes later, while returning home alone, they were attacked by the lone Me-163 who made only one pass before being driven off by friendly P-51 fighters. The report for the "Out House Mouse" indicates that she successfully dropped her 5-1000 lb bomb load on the target and received only 3 small flak holes during the mission.

* During her 139 combat missions, the "Out House Mouse" made 12 trips to Berlin and participated in the final combat mission flown by the 8th Air Force on April 25, 1945 to Pilsen, Czechslovakia.

* She returned to the United States on May 26, 1945. Being "regular army", it was not characteristic of Lt Harvey to argue with those of higher rank. In this instance however he made an exception and protested not being able to fly his assigned aircraft home. Having lost the argument, the "Out House Mouse" actually arrived back in the United States two weeks before her assigned crew did.

* Her final flight was November 30, 1945 to Kingman, Arizona. Scrapped – probably in 1963 – too late for the reconstruction project of Tom and Suzzie Reilly of Kissimmee, Florida. Their restored replica of the "Out House Mouse" is expected to make its maiden flight in late 2002.

[I believe the following letter best explains why the work of these men must never be forgotten. In her letter, Mrs. Katz explained that she thinks Doug Gross is one of the "Ragged Irregulars". – grh]

From: Maurice Rowe <100735.1747@compuserve.com>
To: Joan Katz <pauljoan@qnet.com>
Date: Monday, March 15, 1999 4:25 PM
Subject: Gratitude

Dear Mrs Katz,

My friend, Doug Gross, forwarded your e-mail concerning the passing of your husband, Paul. I trust that you will not object to an Englishman sending condolences, but I was a boy in WW2, a schoolboy bombed out of his home in 1941. Much later I joined the RAF and was posted to Bassingbourn, where I learned of the 91st 'Wray's Ragged Irregulars'. I became interested and much was later privileged to be part of the team which organised the ATC Tower Museum at Bassingbourn and assisted in the 1978 Reunion.

I cannot say that I ever met your husband, but he is one of a group of American servicemen for which we, in the UK and especially England, have much admiration and gratitude. Those of my age group still remember the gentle generosity of those men. They were our big brothers, substitute for our own brothers, in my case, one in the RAF in Burma, the other with the RAF in Libya and Italy. The 'Yanks' gave us sweets (candy) and ice cream, cakes, parties, all of which were unknown in wartime England. More than that, they gave us their broad grins and their time. Greatest of all, they prevented my having to live in a Nazi ruled state.

We shall never forget them.

Sincerely,

Maurice Rowe

[I hope the following short story will give current readers the same sense of the sound and feeling of the beginning of a B-17 combat mission that it gave me. Included with the express permission of George H. Odenwaller – grh]

Pre-Mission
by S/Sgt George H. Odenwaller

Orderly – "O.K., everybody up! It's 4 A.M., chow at 4:30, briefing at 5. Good Luck". He leaves!

I open one eye and look at my watch – he's right, it's 4 A.M. – the lights are on – I'm in the top bunk. Lloyd, my radioman is below. Everyone is bitchin' & belly-achin'.

I jump down, grab my toilet articles from my footlocker, put my socks and shoes on while still in my shorts and T-shirt. I look back at the nice warm sack with straw-bag pillow, and trudge down the hall to the latrine!

Back to bunk A.S.A.P, put on my olive-drab "long-johns", pants and shirt. Make sure you've got your "Good Luck charm (Very important)! Put on B-15 Jacket, grab 2-fresh eggs from my own can & leave the building with crew & others in the dark to walk across the small meadow to the combat Mess Hall.

By this time, if you forgot your fresh eggs & cheese, it's too late to go back. You'll have to eat powdered eggs with ham or French toast; sausage, juice – orange or tomato – coffee or tea with real milk or creamed chipped beef on toast which is known as "shit on a shingle", 2-day old white, whole wheat, or rye bread and butter or jelly. Sometimes even biscuits, etc. Always a non-gaseous menu.

Leaving the Mess Hall & still being dark with 4-inch tall grass wet with dew or also wet with large night-crawlers – yep, fat slimmy worms – very slippery – don't fall down!

Then it's over to briefing for instructions for today's mission. Sit down on wooden benches inside a long nissen hut. Before us, a small stage with a large map of Europe with ribbons attached to show the route of the flight to be taken.

"Attention!"

Stand-up.

"At ease, smoke if you wish." Announces a G-2 officer. Another officer points out our target for today – how long the total flight should be, how many hours we will be on oxygen, where and when we will probably encounter enemy aircraft along with the flak areas and what type of fighter protection we will have; P-51's, P-47's & the colors of the aircraft, when they'll pick us up and when they'll leave us. Also, the route back – it's never the same route back. From his briefing, our navigator will advise us all as to when these things might occur while in flight.

The take off time is posted as is the bomb load, the E.T.A. over the target and the E.T.R. [estimated time of return –grh] home. Then comes weather along with bombing altitude, outside temperature, etc. We all made mental notes or sometimes wrote on the back of your hand!!

"Attention!" shouts someone, "Good Hunting – dismissed"

Outside again, we walk over to the 323rd Squadron hanger to pick up our flight gear – all stuffed into a flight bag. Goggles, helmet with headset, oxygen mask, parka with pants, boots, 2-pc silk electric heated jacket & pants i.e. the "green-hornet suit", electric gloves [the ball-turret isn't heated – grh] and a silk scarf (a "mission scarf" usually handed down to a newer crew member from one who completed his missions). Everyone has his own locker and flying gear fitted to him only and returned to the hanger after each mission where damaged items are replaced. Every item is marked – I was "E-7". Oh yes, and don't forget your chest chute! (which for me, in the ball turret, was almost useless – no room for chutes while in the ball turret). Put most of this on and then climb aboard a "6-by" – a large covered truck – and head for the gun shack to pick up our personal gun barrels.

Then onto the truck again, this time to head across the old Roman Road to where our ground crew and aircraft – "Out House Mouse" awaited us – it's still dark!

Three crews and their flight gear are usually aboard one truck. The driver calls out the pilot's name for each crew who are then delivered to their aircraft. About the same time, the Officer's Jeep arrives and we all meet once again for "another one".

I put my gun barrels down by the ball turret – the rear door of the ball already open thanks to the ground crew. All switches are "On". I flip my master switch "On" for lights and power, remove the gun back-plates and install the gun barrels. Then I replace the back plates, turn off all switches, and close up the turret door – all this while on my knees. The back plates for the .50cal. Machine guns are also known as "buffer plates", containing a 1/8-inch red fiber disc. These discs were usually removed by the gunners and replaced with a U.S. quarter to provide quicker recoil action so the guns fired faster.

It is still dark! We stand outside the aircraft, smoke and bull-shit with the ground crew or go aboard the aircraft to keep warm – no smoking aboard the aircraft while on the ground!

We wait for "Joe" our Pilot to come by inside the aircraft to discuss any possible problems. Take off time is coming up – so we settle down.

Joe goes forward through the radio room and bomb bay and closes the door to the flight deck. We already checked the bomb bay, so Lloyd, the radioman, closes the door to this side of the bomb bay. A few moments later, Joe cranks up the #4 engine and the aircraft begins to vibrate and oscillate – blue smoke blows back past the port waist window while the #2 engine is started up. More noise and bouncing – then the #3 and #1 are also roaring! The engines are then run up, one by one, to maximum rpm (redline) then back down to idle. The magneto are checked, the chocks are pulled from the wheels and the brakes begin to squeal as the aircraft begins to taxi from the revetment and hardstand out to the perimeter track leading to the far end of the runway. We and about 30 other B-17's following each other in the dark, (navigation lights on of course), move, squeal, stop - move, squeal, stop - move, stop, turn right, stop, move – outboard engines revving to high and then low rpm to move us down the track. Finally, our turn off – Joe swings the "Mouse" right with the port engine in high rpm and lines up with the runway.

Then heavy on the brakes! We stand there poised for take off with all 4 engines at their maximum rpm – the aircraft straining and bouncing and waiting to go as Joe is standing on the brakes. Then Joe pushes the throttles fully forward and releases the brakes as the tower says "Go" and we surge forward quickly – the noise here in the waist is deafening. At this point, as we gain speed, if we can get up to look out the port waist window, we see and wave to the 3 "sky pilots" standing alongside the runway, each with his own horseshoe raised high – these 3 sky pilots consisted of a minister, a priest and a Rabbi. We wave as the aircraft vibration stops and now only engine noise prevails as we leave the ground slowly gaining altitude and making a shallow turn to port into the light of dawn.

Now, all eyes are wide and watch for other aircraft around, above and below us while we look for the "form-up" ship up here while circling over the field. We find our position and hang in there until all the aircraft have caught up and are in position. Then the "form-up" ship leaves and as a group, we head for the channel while forming up with other groups!

The "form-up" ship is an old war weary B-17 that has been stripped of all weight – turrets, guns and any excess equipment not needed by a non-combat ship – and painted grossly with strips and polka-dots and outlined with many lights. It carried a crew of four, a pilot, co-pilot, engineer and radioman. I saw it once on the field. It was all white with big red, blue and yellow polka-dots. In the dark, it was an airplane; on the ground in daylight, it was bazaar!

"Ok", says Joe, "light up if you wish" We can smoke before we hit the coast of France while still gaining altitude, from there on it's oxygen time. I crank my turret down so that the access door is in the floor opening, open both door latches and with the guns down my turret is ready for entry. As I step into my ball, the first thing I do is plug my headset into my jack box (radio) and pickup a disk jockey somewhere down there in France in a special services mobile truck who's name was "Sgt Mel Galiard". This was the A.F.N. (Armed Forces Network) and he played all the Big Band music only – Artie Shaw, Tommy Dorsey, Glenn Miller, Benny Goodman, etc. His thing was "Music from down here to someone up there" – boy, was he right. I was all hooked up now – headset, heated suit, all turret and gun-sight switches "on". We are at 10,000 feet now – hook up oxygen mask – set flow to "demand"- pull ball turret door closed, secure both latches. Our waist gunner, Al Kus, checks my door – when "okay" he bangs twice (thanks Al).

I rotate the turret up with the guns now horizontal with the flight of the aircraft and notify Joe (Pilot) that I want to test fire my guns. Everyone else follows. Right now, we are all settled in. Joe calls for an oxygen check: (every 5 minutes), navigator, bombardier, co-pilot, engineer, radio, ball, waist, tail; all in quick succession. Lots of airplanes up here! I rotate – we are on our way!

"Pay attention!" Keep alert, watch for fighters – both German and our own for fighter protection. The morning sky and clouds are beautiful – the engines drone on and vibrate – very relaxing.

"I wonder", I wonder, "my God – what am I doing up here ?"

George Odenwaller
Ball Turret Gunner – 26 Missions
91st B.G., 323rd B.S., Bassingbourn, Cambs., England.
A/C No 231636, "Outhouse Mouse" – Call Letters, OR N – 139 Missions on a/c

AIRCREW WINGS

Drawing Courtesy G.H. Odenwaller

BOMBARDIER

2ND LT. MARTIN J. RABER

NAVIGATOR

2ND LT. PAUL KATZ

PILOT

1ST LT. ELMER J. HRVEY

CO-PILOT

2ND LT. PHIL DARBY

ENGINEER-GUNNER

S/SGT. NEIL C. JORGENSON

RADIO-GUNNER

S/SGT. MILTON H. LLOYD

BALL GUNNER

S/SGT. GEO. H. ODENWALLER

WAIST GUNNER

S/SGT. ELMER A. KUS

TAIL GUNNER

S/SGT. WALTER M. LIMBERGER

BIBLIOGRAPHY & CREDITS

Reference sources used for information related to specific aircraft mentioned in the diaries:

The Ragged Irregulars of Bassingbourn, The 91st Bombardment Group in World War II, by Marion H. Havelaar. Published by Schiffer Publishing Ltd., 1995.

Plane Names & Fancy Noses, Vol I, The 91st Bomb Group (Heavy), United States Army Airforce, Bassingbourn, England, 1942-1945, by Ray Bowden. Published in England by Design Oracle Partnership, 1993. "Outhouse Mouse" pages 159-161.

Regarding the Pilsen raid:

The Last Mission of the 91st – Pandemonium Over Pilsen: The Forgotten Final Mission, by Lowell L. Getz, copyright 1997. Located on the website of the 91st Bomb Group at:
                    http:/www.91stbombgroup.com/lastmission.html

Front Cover: Nose-Art and B-17 graphic courtesy of George H. Odenwaller.
Back Cover : Insignia graphic courtesy of www.91stbombgroup.com

SOURCES for ADDITIONAL INFORMATION

For those who have Internet capability, the following websites may be of interest:

http://www.91stbombgroup.com
http://www.b-17combatcrewmen.org

Both of these websites have numerous links to other interesting sites and items including photographs, stories, diaries, bulletin boards and much more. I encourage everyone with the capability to do so, to browse both of these wonderful websites.

[I pray that all of these men, living and dead, who made this world safe for my generation and my descendents, may finally rest with their God in everlasting peace. – grh]

As a small boy, Robert Harvey's interest in the small red leather diary with the brass buckle was usually met with a slap on the hands and the admonishment that he would be told about the book when he was old enough to understand. As stated in his introduction, his father died before Bob was able to learn the facts of the book first hand, but through his research and the collection of the diaries of the other members of his father's B-17 crew, that small book is now available to anyone interested enough to open the cover of this book. Those who do will be able to see and read the combined recollections of this one crew exactly as they were written immediately following their missions over Germany.

Born in Boone, Iowa in April, 1945, Bob is the second of four children. Following his active duty service in the United States Air Force during the Viet Nam War, Bob graduated as an electrical engineer and has worked for a major west coast utility company for over 30 years. He currently lives in northern California.

Printed in the United States
by Baker & Taylor Publisher Services